How to Develope
Self-Confidence
and Improve
Public Speaking

BESTSELLING NON-FICTION

- Gravity by George Gamow
  Sciences/Physics, ISBN: 9789388118705

- How to Develop Self-Confi. and Pub. Speaking by Dale Carnegie
  Mind, Body & Spirit, ISBN: 9789388118286

- How to Stop Worrying and Start Living by Dale Carnegie
  Mind, Body & Spirit, ISBN: 9789387669161

- How to Win Friends and Influence People by Dale Carnegie
  Self Help/General, ISBN: 9789387669178

- Mein Kampf by Adolf Hitler
  Autobiographies/Leaders, ISBN: 9789387669260

- My Experiments with Truth by Mahatma Gandhi
  Autobiographies/Leaders, ISBN: 9789387669277

- Relativity by Albert Einstein
  Sciences/Physics, ISBN: 9789387669185

- The Art of War by Sun Tzu
  Self Help/Success, ISBN: 9789387669321

- The Diary of a Young Girl by Anne Frank
  Autobiographies/Memoirs, ISBN: 9789387669208

- The Magic of Believing by Claudie Bristol
  Religion/Christianity, ISBN: 9789388118217

- The Miracles of Your Mind by Joseph Murphy
  Mind, Body & Spirit, ISBN: 9789387669215

- The Power of Your Subconscious Mind by Joseph Murphy
  Mind, Body & Spirit, ISBN: 9789387669222

- The Richest Man in Babylon by George S. Clason
  Business & Economics, ISBN: 9789388118354

- Think and Grow Rich by Napoleon Hill
  Self Help/Success, ISBN: 9789387669352

HOW TO DEVELOPE SELF-CONFIDENCE AND IMPROVE PUBLIC SPEAKING

TIME-TESTED METHODS OF PERSUASION

DALE CARNEGIE

gp

GENERAL PRESS

Published by
GENERAL PRESS
4805/24, Fourth Floor, Krishna House
Ansari Road, Daryaganj, New Delhi - 110002
Ph : 011-23282971, 45795759
E-mail : generalpressindia@gmail.com

www.generalpress.in

First Edition : 2018
Revised Edition : 2019

ISBN : 9789388118286

Published by Azeem Ahmad Khan for General Press

Contents

Dale Carnegie

Dale Carnegie (1888–1955) was an American writer and lecturer and the developer of famous courses in self-improvement, salesmanship, corporate training, public speaking and interpersonal skills.

He was born in an impoverished family in Maryville, Missouri. Carnegie harbored a strong love and passion for public speaking from a very early age and was very proactive in debate in high school. He went to the Warrensburg State Teachers College and later onwards became a salesman for Armour and Company in Nebraska. He also moved to New York in the pursuit of a career in acting and gave classes in public speaking at the Young Men's Christian Association.

During the early 1930's, he was renowned and very famous for his books and a radio program. *When How to Win Friends and Influence People* was published in 1930. It became an instant success and subsequently became one of the biggest bestsellers of all time. It sold more than 10 million copies in many different languages. He also began work as a newspaper columnist and formed the Dave Carnegie Institute for Effective Speaking and Human Relations, with several branches globally.

Carnegie loved teaching others to climb the pillars of success. His valuable and tested advice was used in many domains and has been the inspiration of many famous people's success. One of the core ideas in his books is that it is possible to change other people's behavior by changing one's reaction to them. The most famous and cited maxims in the book are "Believe that you will succeed, and you will," and "Learn to love, respect and enjoy other people."

....

Increase Courage and Self-Confidence

"Courage is one step ahead of fear."

—Coleman Young

More than eighteen thousand businesspersons, since 1912, have been members of the various public speaking courses conducted by me. Most of them have, at my request, written stating why they had enrolled for this training and what they hoped to obtain from it. Naturally, the phraseology varied; but the central desire in these letters, the basic want in the vast majority, remained surprisingly the same: "When I am called upon to stand up and speak," man after man wrote, "I become so self-conscious, so frightened, that I can't think clearly, can't concentrate, can't remember what I had intended to say. I want to gain self-confidence, poise, and the ability to think on my feet. I want to get my thoughts together in logical order and I want to be able to say my say clearly and convincingly before a business group or audience." Thousands of their confessions sounded about like that. Years ago, a gentleman here called D.W. Ghent joined my public speaking course in Philadelphia. Shortly after the opening session, he invited me to lunch with him in the Manufacturers' Club. He was a man of middle age and had always led an active life; was head of his own manufacturing establishment, a leader in church work and civic activities. While we were having lunch that day, he leaned across the table and said: "I have been asked many times to talk before various gatherings but I have never been able to do so. I get so fussed, my mind becomes an utter blank: so I have side-stepped it all my life. But I am chairman now of a board of college trustees. I must preside at their meetings. Do you think it will be possible for me to learn to speak at this late date in my life?"

"Do I *think*, Mr. Ghent?" I replied. "It is *not* a question of my *thinking*. I *know you can,* and I *know you will* if you will only practice and follow the directions and instructions."

After he had completed his training, we lost touch with each other for a while. In 1921, we met and lunched together again at the Manufacturers' Club. We sat in the same corner and occupied the same table that we had had on the first occasion. Reminding him of our former conversation, I asked him if I had been too sanguine then. He took a little red-backed notebook out of his pocket and showed me a list of talks and dates for which he was booked. "And the ability to make these," he confessed, "the pleasure I get in doing it, the additional service I can render to the community—these are among the most gratifying things in my life."

The International Conference for the Limitation of Armaments had been held in Washington shortly before that. When it was known that Lloyd George was planning to attend it, the Baptists of Philadelphia cabled, inviting him to speak at a great mass meeting to be held in their city. Lloyd George cabled back that if he came to Washington he would accept their invitation. And Mr. Ghent informed me that he himself had been chosen, from among all the Baptists of that city, to introduce England's premier to the audience.

And this was the man who had sat at that same table less than three years before and solemnly asked me if I thought he would ever be able to talk in public!

Was the rapidity with which he forged ahead in his speaking ability unusual? Not at all. There have been hundreds of similar cases. For example—to quote one more specific instance—years ago, a Brooklyn physician, whom we will call Dr. Curtis, spent the winter in Florida near the training grounds of the Giants. Being an enthusiastic baseball fan, he often went to see them practise. In time, he became quite friendly with the team, and was invited to attend a banquet given in their honour.

After the coffee and nuts were served, several prominent guests were called upon to "say a few words". Suddenly with the abruptness and unexpectedness of an explosion, he heard the toast-master remark: "We have a physician with us tonight, and I am going to ask Dr. Curtis to talk on a baseball player's health."

Was he prepared? Of course. He had had the best preparation in the world; he had been studying hygiene and practising medicine for almost a third of a century. He could have sat in his chair and talked about this subject all night to the man seated on his right or left. But to get up and say the same things to even a small audience—that was another matter. That was a paralyzing matter. His heart doubled its pace and skipped beats at the very contemplation of it. He had never made a public speech in his life, and every thought he had had now took wings.

What was he to do? The audience was applauding. Everyone was looking at him. He shook his head. But that served only to heighten the applause, to increase the demand. The cries of "Dr. Curtis! Speech! Speech!" grew louder and more insistent.

He was in positive misery. He knew that if he got up he would fail, that he would be unable to utter half a dozen sentences. So he arose and, without saying a word, turned his back on his friends and walked silently out of the room, a deeply embarrassed and humiliated man.

Small wonder that one of the first things he did after getting back to Brooklyn was to come to the Central Y.M.C.A. and enrol in the course in Public Speaking. He didn't propose to be put to the blush and be stricken dumb a second time.

He was the kind of student that delights an instructor: he was in dead earnest. He wanted to be able to talk, and there was no half-heartedness about his desires. He prepared his talks thoroughly, he practised them with a will, and he never missed a single session of the course.

He did precisely what such a student always does: he progressed at a rate that surprised him, that surpassed his fondest hopes. After the first few sessions his nervousness subsided, and his confidence mounted higher and higher. In two months he had become the star speaker of the group. He was soon accepting invitations to speak elsewhere; he now loved the feel and exhilaration of it, the distinction and the additional friends it brought him.

The gaining of self-confidence and courage and the ability to think calmly and clearly while talking to a group is not one-tenth as difficult as most men imagine. It is not a gift bestowed by providence on only a few rarely endowed individuals. It is like the ability to play golf. Any man can develop his own latent capacity if he has sufficient desire to do so.

Is there the faintest shadow of a reason why you should not be able to think as well in a perpendicular position before an audience as you can when sitting down? Surely, you know there is not. In fact, you ought to think better when facing a group of men. Their presence ought to stir you and lift you. A great many speakers will tell you that the presence of an audience is a stimulus, an inspiration, that drives their brains to function more clearly, more keenly. At such times, thoughts, facts, ideas, that they did not know they possessed, drift smoking by, as Henry Ward Beecher said; and they have but to reach out and lay their hands hot upon them. They ought to be your experience. It probably will be if you practise and persevere.

Of this much, however, you may be absolutely sure: training and practise will wear away your audience-fright and give you self-confidence and an abiding courage.

Do not imagine that your case is unusually difficult. Even those who afterwards became the most eloquent representatives of their generation were, at the outset of their careers, afflicted by this blinding fear and self-consciousness.

Mark Twain, the first time he stood up to lecture, felt as if his mouth were filled with cotton and his pulse were speeding for some prize cup.

The late Jean Jaurès, the most powerful political speaker that France produced during his generation, sat, for a year, tongue-tied in the Chamber of Deputies before he could summon of the courage to make his initial speech.

John Bright, the illustrious Englishman who, during the civil war, defended in England the cause of union and emancipation, made his maiden speech before a group of countryfolk gathered in a school building. He was so frightened on the way to the place, so fearful that he would fail, that he implored his companion to start applause to bolster him up whenever he showed signs of giving way to his nervousness.

Charles Stewart Parnell, the great Irish leader, at the outset of his speaking career, was so nervous, according to the testimony of his brother, that he frequently clenched his fists until his nails sank into his flesh and his palms bled.

Disraeli admitted that he would rather have led a cavalry charge than have faced the House of Commons for the first time. His opening speech there was a ghastly failure. So was Sheridan's.

In fact, so many of the famous speakers of England have made poor showings at first that there is now a feeling in Parliament that it is rather an inauspicious omen for a young man's initial talk to be a decided success. So take heart.

After watching the careers and aiding somewhat in the development of so many speakers, the author is always glad when a student has, at the outset, a certain amount of flutter and nervous agitation.

There is a certain responsibility in making a talk, even if it is to only two dozen men in a business conference—a certain strain, a certain shock, a certain excitement. The speaker ought to be keyed up like a thoroughbred straining of the bit. The immortal Cicero said, two thousand years ago, that all public speaking of real merit was characterized by nervousness.

Speakers often experience this same feeling even when they are talking over the radio. "Microphone fright", it is called. When Charlie Chaplin went "on the air", he had his speech all written out. Surely he was used to audiences. He toured America back in 1912 with a vaudeville sketch entitled "A Night in a Music Hall". Before that he was on the legitimate stage in England. Yet, when he went into the padded room and faced the microphone, he had a feeling in the stomach not unlike the sensation one gets when he crosses the Atlantic during a stormy February.

James Kirkwood, a famous motion picture actor and director, had a similar experience. He used to be a star on the speaking stage; but when he came out of the sending room after addressing the invisible audience, he was mopping perspiration from his brow. "An opening night on Broadway," he confessed, "is nothing in comparison to that."

Some men, no matter how often they speak, always experience this self-consciousness just before they commence; but in a few seconds after they have got on their feet, it disappears.

Even Lincoln felt shy for the few opening moments. In a few moments he gained composure and warmth and earnestness, and his real speech began.

Your experience may be similar to his.

In order to get the most out of this training, and to get it with rapidity and dispatch, four things are essential:

FIRST
START WITH A STRONG AND PERSISTENT DESIRE

This is of far more importance than you probably realize. If your instructor could look into your mind and heart now and ascertain the depth of your desires, he could foretell, almost with certainty, the swiftness of the progress you will make. If your desire is pale and flabby, your achievements will also take on that hue and consistency. But, if you go after this subject with persistence, and with the energy of a bulldog after a cat, nothing underneath the Milky Way will defeat you.

Therefore, arouse your enthusiasm for this study. Enumerate its benefits. Think of what additional self-confidence and the ability to talk more convincingly in business will mean to you. Think of what it may mean to you socially; of the friends it will bring, of the increase of your personal influence, of the leadership it will give you. And it will give you leadership more rapidly than almost any other activity you can think of or imagine.

It is an attainment that almost every person of education longs for. After Andrew Carnegie's death there was found, among his papers, a plan for his life drawn up when he was thirty-three years of age. He then felt that in two more years he could so arrange his business as to have an annual income of fifty thousand dollars; so he proposed to retire at thirty-five, go to Oxford and get a thorough education, and *"pay special attention to speaking in public."*

Think of the glow of satisfaction and pleasure that will accrue from the exercise of this new power. The author has travelled round over no small part of this terrestrial ball; and has had many and varied experiences;

but for downright, and lasting inward satisfaction, he knows of few things that will compare to standing before an audience and making men think your thoughts after you. It will give you a sense of strength, a feeling of power. It will appeal to your pride of personal accomplishment. It will set you off from and raise you above your fellowmen. There is magic in it and a never-to-be-forgotten thrill. "Two minutes before I begin," a speaker confessed, "I would rather be whipped than start; but two minutes before I finish, I would rather be shot than stop."

In every course, some men grow faint-hearted and fall by the wayside; so you should keep thinking of what this course will mean to you until your desire is white hot. You should start this programme with an enthusiasm that will carry you through every session, triumphant to the end. Tell your friends that you have joined this course. Set aside one certain night of the week for the reading of these lessons and the preparation of your talks. In short, make it as easy as possible to go ahead. Make it as difficult as possible to retreat.

When Julius Ceasar sailed over the channel from Gaul and landed with his legions on what is now England, what did he do to insure the success of his arms? A very clever thing: he halted his soldiers on the chalk cliffs of Dover, and, looking down over the waves two hundred feet below, they saw red tongues of fire consume every ship in which they had crossed. In the enemy's country, with the last link with the Continent gone, the last means of retreating burned, there was but one thing left for them to do: to advance, to conquer. That is precisely what they did.

Such was the spirit of the immortal Caesar. Why not make it yours, too, in this war to exterminate your foolish fear of audiences.

SECOND

ACT CONFIDENTLY

To develop courage when you are facing an audience, act as if you already have it. Of course, unless you are prepared, all the acting in the world will avail but little. But granted that you know what you are going to talk about, step out briskly and take a deep breath. In fact, breathe deeply for thirty seconds before you ever face your audience. The increased supply of oxygen will buoy you up and give you courage. The great tenor, Jean de Reszke, used to say that when you had your breath so you "could sit on it", nervousness vanished.

When a youth of the Peuhl tribe in Central Africa attains manhood and wishes to take unto himself a wife, he is compelled to undergo the ceremony of flagellation. The women of the tribe foregather, singing and clapping their hands to the rhythm of tom-toms. The candidate strides forth stripped naked to the waist. Suddenly a man armed with a cruel whip sets upon the lad, beating his bare skin, lashing him, flogging him like a fiend. Welts appear; often the skin is cut, blood flows; scars are made that last a lifetime. During this scourging, a venerable judge of the tribe crouches at the feet of the victim to see if he moves or exhibits the slightest evidence of pain. To pass the test successfully the tortured aspirant must not only endure the ordeal, but, as he endures it, he must sing a paean of praise.

In every age, in every clime, men have always admired courage; so, no matter how your heart may be pounding inside, stride forth bravely, stop, stand still like the scourged youth of Central Africa, and like him, act as if you loved it.

Draw yourself up to your full height and look your audience straight in the eyes, and begin to talk as confidently as if every one of them owed you money. Imagine that they do. Imagine that they have assembled there to bet you for an extension of credit. The psychological effect on you will be beneficial.

Do not nervously button and unbutton your coat, and fumble with your hands. If you must make nervous movements, place your hands behind your back and twist your fingers there where no one can see the performance—or wiggle your toes.

As a general rule, it is bed for a speaker to hide behind furniture, but it may give you a little courage the first few times to stand behind a table or chair and to grip them tightly—or hold a coin firmly in the palm of your hand.

How did Theodore Roosevelt develop his characteristic courage and self-reliance? Was he endowed by nature with a venturesome and daring spirit? Not at all. "Having been a rather sickly and awkward boy," he confesses in his *Autobiography*. "I was, as a young man, at first both nervous and distrustful of my own prowess. I had to train myself painfully and laboriously not merely as regards my body but as regards my soul and spirit."

Fortunately, he has told us how he achieved the transformation: "When a boy," he writes, "I read a passage in one of Marryat's books which always impressed me. In this passage the captain of some small British man-of-war is explaining to the hero how to acquire the quality of fearlessness. He says that at the outset almost every man is frightened when he goes into action, but that the course to follow is for the man to keep such a grip on himself that he can act just if he were not frightened. After this is kept up long enough, it changes from pretence to reality, and the man does in very fact become fearless by sheer dint of practising fearlessness when he does not feel it. (I am using my own language, not Marryat's.)

"This was the theory upon which I went. There were all kinds of things of which I was afraid at first, ranging from grizzly bears to 'mean' horses and gun-fighters; but by acting as if I was not afraid I gradually ceased to be afraid. Most men can have the same experience if they choose."

So take the offensive against your fears. Go out to meet them, battle them, conquer them by sheer boldness at every opportunity.

Have a massage, and then think of yourself as a courier boy instructed to deliver it. We pay slight attention to the boy. It is the courier that we want. The message—that is the thing. Keep your mind on it. Keep your heart in it. Know it like the back of your hand. Believe it feelingly. Then talk as if you were determined to say it. Do that, and the chances are ten to one that you will soon be master of the occasion and master of yourself.

THIRD
KNOW THOROUGHLY WHAT YOU ARE GOING TO TALK ABOUT

Unless a man has thought out and planned his talk and knows what he is going to say, he can't feel very comfortable when he faces his auditors. He is like the blind leading the blind. Under such circumstances, your speaker ought to be self-conscious, ought to feel repentant, ought to be ashamed of his negligence.

"I was elected to the Legislature in the autumn of 1881," Theodore Roosevelt wrote in his *Autobiography,* "and found myself the youngest man in that body. Like all young men and inexperienced members, I had considerable difficulty in teaching myself to speak. I profited much by the advice of a hard-headed old countryman—who was unconsciously paraphrasing the Duke of Wellington, who was himself doubtless paraphrasing somebody else. The advice ran: 'Don't speak until you are sure you have something to say, and know just what it is; then say it, and sit down.'"

This "hard-headed old countryman" ought to have told Roosevelt of another aid in overcoming nervousness. He ought to have added: "It will help you to throw off your embarrassment if you can find something to do before an audience—if you can exhibit something, write a word on the blackboard or point out a spot on the map, or move a table or throw open a window, or shift some books and papers—any physical action with a purpose behind it may help you to feel more at home."

True it is not always easy to find an excuse for doing such things, but there is the suggestion. Use it if you can, but use it the first few times only. A baby does not cling to chairs after it learns to walk.

FOURTH
PRACTISE! PRACTISE! PRACTISE!

The last point we have to make here is emphatically the most important. Even though you forget everything you have read so far, do remember this: the first way, the last way, the never-failing way to develop self-confidence in speaking is—to speak. Really the whole matter finally simmers down to but one essential: practise, practise, practise. That is the *sine qua non* of it all, "the without which not".

"Any beginner," warned Roosevelt, "is apt to have 'buck fever'. 'Buck fever' means a state of intense nervous excitement which may be entirely divorced from timidity. It may affect a man the first time he has to speak to a large audience just as it may affect him the first time he sees a buck-deer or goes into battle. What such a man needs is not courage, but nerve control and cool-headedness. This he can get only by actual practice. He must, by custom and repeated exercise of self-mastery, get his nerves thoroughly under control. This is largely a matter of habit; in the sense of repeated effort and repeated exercise of willpower. If the man has the tight stuff in him, he will grow stronger and stronger with each exercise of it."

So, persevere. Don't remain away from any session of the course because the business duties of the week have rendered it impossible for you to prepare something. Prepared or unprepared, come. Let the instructor, the class, suggest a topic for you after you have come before them.

You want to get rid of your audience fear? Let us see what causes it.

Fear is the result of a lack of confidence and what causes that? It is the result of not knowing what you can really do. And not knowing what you can do is caused by a lack of experience. When you get a record of successful experience behind you, your fears will vanish; they will melt like night mists under the glare of a July sun.

One thing is certain: the accepted way to learn to swim is to plunge into the water. You have been reading this book long enough. Let as toss it aside now, and get busy with the real work in hand.

Choose your subject, preferably one on which you have some knowledge, and construct at three-minute talk. Practise the talk by yourself a number of times. Then give it, if possible, to the group for whom it is intended, or before your class, putting into the effort all your force and power.

> *"It is never easy to keep reaching for dreams.*
> *Strength and courage can sometimes be lonely*
> *friends. But those who reach, walk in stardust."*
>
> **—Anonymous**

> *"Healing takes courage, and we all have courage,*
> *even if we have to dig a little to find it."*
>
> **—Tori Amos**

··

How to Open a Talk

"You have to care. And that care has to come
from your soul Public speaking is the art of having
everybody thinking you are talking to them."

—Dennis Van Gerven

I once asked Dr. Lynn Harold Hough, formerly president of Northwestern University, what was the most important fact that his long experience as a speaker had taught him. After pondering for a minute, he replied, "To get an arresting opening, something that will seize the attention immediately." He plans in advance almost the precise words of both his opening and closing. John Bright did the same thing. Gladstone did it. Webster did it. Lincoln did it. Practically every speaker with common sense and experience does it.

But does the beginner? Seldom. Planning takes time, requires thought, demands willpower. Cerebration is a painful process. Thomas Edison had this quotation from Sir Joshua Reynolds nailed on the walls of his plants:

"There is no expedient to which a man will not resort to avoid the real labour of thinking."

The tyro usually trusts to the inspiration of the moment with the consequence that he finds:

"Beset with pitfall and with gin,

The road he is to wander in."

The late Lord Northcliffe, who fought his way up from a meagre weekly salary to being the richest and most influential newspaper owner in the British Empire, said that these five words from Pascal had done more to help him succeed than anything else he had ever read:

"To foresee is to rule."

That is also a most excellent motto to have on your desk when you are planning your talk. Foresee how you are going to begin when the mind is fresh to grasp every word you utter. Foresee what impression you are going to leave last—when nothing else follows to obliterate it.

Ever since the days of Aristotle, books on this subject have divided the speech into three sections: the introduction, the body, the conclusion. Until comparatively recently, the introduction often was, and could really afford to be, as leisurely as a cart ride. The speaker then was both a bringer of news and an entertainer. A hundred years ago he often filled the niche in the community that is usurped today by the newspaper, the radio, the telephone, the movie theatre.

But conditions have altered amazingly. The world has been made over. Inventions have speeded up life more in the last hundred years than they had formerly in all the ages since Belshazzar and Nebuchadnezzar. Automobiles, aeroplanes, radio; we are moving with increasing speed. And the speaker must fall in line with the impatient tempo of the times. If you are going to use an introduction, believe me, it ought to be short as a billboard advertisement. This is about the temper of the average modern audience: "Got anything to say? All right, let's have it quickly and with very little trimmings. No oratory! Give us the facts quickly and sit down."

When Woodrow Wilson addressed Congress on such a momentous question as an ultimatum on submarine warfare, he announced his topic and centred the audience's attention on the subject with just twenty-three words:

"A situation has arisen in the foreign relations of the country of which it is my plain duty to inform you very frankly."

The salesmanager for the National Cash Register Company opened one of his talks to his men in this fashion. Only three sentences in this introduction; and they are all easy to listen to, they all have vigour and drive:

"You man who get the orders are the chaps who are supposed to keep the smoke coming out of the factory chimney. The volume of smoke emitted from our chimney during the past two summer months hasn't been large enough to darken the landscape to any great extent. Now that the dog days are over and the business-revival season has begun, we are addressing to you a short, sharp request on this subject: We want more smoke."

But do inexperienced speakers usually achieve such commendable swiftness and succinctness in their openings? Strict veracity compels us to record that they do not. The majority of untrained and unskilled speakers will begin in one of two ways—both of which are bed. Let us discuss them forthwith.

THE PITFALLS OF OPENING WITH A SO-CALLED HUMOROUS STORY

For some lamentable reason, the novice often feels that he ought to be funny as a speaker. He may, by nature, mind you, be as solemn as the encyclopædia, utterly devoid of the lighter touch, yet the moment he stands up to talk he imagines he feels, or ought to feel, the spirit of Mark Twain descending upon him. So he is inclined to open with a humorous story, especially if the occasion is an after-dinner affair. What happens? The chances are twenty to one that the narration, the manner of this hardware merchant newly-turned raconteur, is as heavy as the dictionary. The chances are his stories don't "click". In the immortal language of the immortal Hamlet, they prove "weary, stale, flat and unprofitable".

If an entertainer were to misfire a few times like that before a vaude-ville audience that had paid for their seats, they would "boo" and shout "give him the bird". But the average group listening to a speaker is very sympathetic; so, out of sheer charity, they will do their best to manufac-ture a few chuckles while, deep in their hearts, they pity the would-be humorous speaker for his failure! They themselves feel uncomfortable. Haven't you, my dear reader, witnessed this kind of fiasco time after time?

The write has. In all the difficult realm of speech-making what is more difficult, more rare, than the ability to make an audience laugh? Humour is a hair-trigger affair; it is so much a matter of individuality, of personality. You are either born with the predilection for being humorous or you are not—much as you are born with or without brown eyes. Not much can be done about either.

Remember, it is seldom the story that is funny of, by, and in itself. It is the way it is told that makes it a success. Ninety-nine men out of a hundred will fail woefully with the identical stories that made Mark Twain famous. Read the stories that Lincoln repeated in the taverns of the English Judicial District of Illinois, stories that men drove miles to hear, stories that men sat up all night to hear, stories that, according to an eye witness, sometimes caused the natives to "whoop and roll off their chairs". Read those stories aloud to your family and see if you conjure up a smile. Here is one Lincoln used to tell with roaring success. Why not try it? Privately, please—not before an audience. A late traveller, trying to reach home over the muddy roads of the Illinois prairies, was overtaken by a storm. The night was black as ink, the rain descended as if some dam in the heavens had broken, thunder rent the angry clouds like the explosion of dynamite. Chain lightning showed trees falling around. The roar of it was very nearly deafening. Finally a crash more terrific, more terrible than any the helpless man had ever heard in his life, brought him to his knees. He was not given to praying usually, but "Oh, Lord," he gasped, "if it is all the same to you, please give us a little more light and a little less noise."

You may be one of those fortunately endowed individuals who has the rare gift of humour. If so, by all means, cultivate it. You will be thrice welcome wherever you speak. But if you talent lies in other directions, it is folly—and it ought to be high treason—for you to attempt to wear the mantle of Chauncey M. Depew.

Were you to study his speeches, and Lincoln's, and job Hedges', you would probably be surprised at the few stories they told, especially in their openings. Edwin James Cattell confided to me that he had never told a funny story for the mere sake of humour. It had to be relevant, had to illustrate a point. Humour ought to be merely the frosting on the cake, merely the chocolate between the layers, not the cake itself. Strickland Gillilan, the best humorous lecturer, makes it a rule never to tell a story during the first three minutes of his talk. If he finds that practise advisable, I wonder if you and I would not also.

Must the opening then be heavy-footed, elephantine and excessively solemn? Not at all. Tickle our visibilities, if you can, by some local reference, something anent the occasion or the remarks of some other speaker. Observe some incongruity. Exaggerate it. That brand of humour is forty times more likely to succeed than stale jokes about Pat and Mike, or a mother-in-law, or a goat.

Perhaps the easiest way to create merriment is to tell a joke on yourself. Depict yourself in some ridiculous and embarrassing situation. That gets down to the very essence of much humour. The Eskimos laugh even at a chap who has broken his leg. The Chinese chuckle over the dog that has fallen out of a second storey window and killed himself. We are a bit more sympathetic than that, but don't we smile at the fellow chasing his hat, or slipping on a banana skin?

Almost anyone can make an audience laugh by grouping incongruous ideas of qualities as, for example, the statement of a newspaper writer that he "hated children, tripe, and Democrats".

Note how cleverly Rudyard Kipling raised laughs in this opening to one of his talks in England. He is retailing here, not manufactured anecdotes, but some of his own experiences and playfully stressing their incongruities:

> My Lords. Ladies and Gentlemen: When I was a young man in India I used to report criminal cases for the newspaper that employed me. It was interesting work because it introduced me to forgers and embezzlers and murderers and enterprising sportsmen of that kind. (Laughter.) Sometimes, after I had reported their trials, I used to visit my friends in jail when they were doing their sentences. (Laughter.) I remember one man who got off with a life sentence for murder. He was a clever, smooth-speaking chap, and he told me what he called the story of his life. He said: "Take it from me that when a man gets crooked, one thing leads to another until he finds himself in such a position that he has to put somebody out of the way to get straight again." (Laughter.)

Well, that exactly describes the present position of the cabinet. (Laughter and cheers.)

This is the way William Howard Taft managed a bit of humour at the annual banquet of the superintendents of the Metropolitan Life Insurance Company. The beautiful part of it is this: he is humorous and pays his audience a gracious compliment at the same time:

Mr. President and Gentlemen of the Metropolitan Life Insurance Company:

I was out in my old home about nine months ago, and I heard an after-dinner speech there by a gentleman who had some trepidation in making it; and he said he had consulted a friend of his, who had had a great deal of experience in making after-dinner speeches, which friend advised him that the best kind of audience to address, as an after-dinner speaker, was an audience intelligent and well-educated but half-tight. (Laughter and applause.) Now, all I can say is that this audience is one of the best audiences I ever saw for an after-dinner speaker. Something has made up for the absence of that element that the remark implied (applause), and I must think it is the spirit of the Metropolitan Life Insurance Company. (Prolonged applause.)

DON'T BE APOLOGETIC

The second egregious blunder that the beginner is wont to make in his opening, is this: he apologizes. "I am no speaker... I am not prepared to talk.... I have nothing to say...?

Don't! Don't! The opening words of a poem by Kipling are: "There's no use in going further." That is precisely the way an audience feels when a speaker opens in that fashion.

Anyway, if you are not prepared, some of us will discover it without your assistance. Others will not. Why call their attention to it? Why insult your audience by suggesting that you did not think them worth preparing for, that just any old thing you happened to have on the fire would be good enough to serve them? No. No. We don't want to hear your apologies. We are there to be informed and interested, to be *interested*, remember that.

The moment you come before the audience, you have our attention naturally, inevitably. It is not difficult to get it for the first five seconds, but it is difficult to hold it for the next five minutes. If you once lose it, it will be doubly difficult to win it back. So begin with something interesting in your very first sentence. Not the second. Not this third. The first! F-I-R-S-T. First!

"How?" you ask. Rather a large order, I admit. And in attempting to harvest the material to fill it, we must tread our way down devious and dubious paths, for so much depends upon you, upon your audience, your subject, your material, the occasion, and so on. However, we hope that the tentative suggestions discussed and Illustrated in the remainder of this chapter will yield something usable and of value.

CURIOSITY WINS OVER THE CAT

Here is an opening used by Mr. Howell Healy in a talk given before a session of this course. Do you like it? Does it get your interest immediately?

Eighty-two years ago, and just about this time of year, there was published in London a little volume, a story, which was destined to become immortal. Many people have called it "the greatest little book in the world". When it first appeared, friends meeting one another in the Strand or Pall Mall, asked the question, "Have you read it?" The answer invariably was: "Yes, God bless him, I have."

The day it was published a thousand copies were sold. Within a fortnight, the demand had consumed fifteen thousand. Since then it has run into countless editions, and has been translated into every language under heaven. A few years ago, J.P. Morgan purchased the original manuscript for a fabulous sum; it now reposes among his other priceless treasures in that magnificent art gallery which he called his library.

What is this world-famous book? Dickens' *A Christmas Carol*....

Do you consider that a successful opening? Did it hold your attention, heighten your interest as it progressed? Why? Was it not because it aroused your curiosity, held you in suspense?

Curiosity! Who is not susceptible to it?

I have seen birds in the woods fly about by the hour watching me out of sheer curiosity. I know a hunter in the high Alps who lures chamois by throwing a bed sheet around him and crawling about and arousing their curiosity. Dogs have curiosity, and so have kittens, and all manner of animals including the well-known *genus homo*.

So arouse your audience's curiosity with your first sentence, and you have their interested attention.

The writer used to begin his lecture on Colonel Thomas Lawrence's adventures in Arabia in this fashion:

"Lloyd George says that he regards Colonel Lawrence as one of the most romantic and picturesque characters of modern times."

That opening had two advantages. In the first place, a quotation from an eminent man always has a lot of attention value. Second, it aroused curiosity: "Why romantic?" was the natural question, and "why picturesque?" "I never heard about him before.... What did he do?"

Lowell Thomas began his lecture on Colonel Thomas Lawrence with this statement:

"I was going down Christian Street in Jerusalem one day when I met a man clad in the gorgeous robes of an oriental potentate: and, at his side, hung the curved gold sword worn only by the descendants of the prophet Mohammed. But this man had none of the appearances of an Arab. He had blue eyes; and the Arabs' eyes are always black or brown."

That piques your curiosity, doesn't it? You want to hear more. Who was he? Why was he posing as an Arab? What did he do? What became of him?

The student who opened his talk with this question: "Do you know that slavery exists in seventeen nations of the world today?" not only aroused curiosity, but in addition, he shocked his auditors. "Slavery? Today? Seventeen countries? Seems incredible. What nations? Where are they?"

One can often arouse curiosity by beginning with an effect, and making people anxious to hear the cause. For example, one student began with this striking statement: "A member of one of our state legislatures recently stood up in his legislative assembly and proposed the passage of a law prohibiting tadpoles from becoming frogs within two miles of any school house."

You smile. Is the speaker joking? How absurd. Was that actually done? Yes. The speaker went on to explain:

> Every man who aspires to speak in public ought to study the technique that magazine writers employ to hook the reader's interest immediately. You can learn far more from them about how to open a speech than you can by studying collections of printed speeches.

WHY NOT BEGIN WITH A STORY

Harold Bell Wright has admitted in an interview that his novels brought him more than a hundred thousand dollars a year. Booth Tarkington and Robert W. Chambers earned similar amounts. For seventeen years Doubleday Page and Company had one large press, which did nothing in all that time but turn out a ceaseless flood of the novels by the late Gene Stratton Porter. Over seventeen million copies of her books were sold, and they brought her more than three million dollars in royalties. Do people like to hear stories? Those figures sound like it, don't they?

We especially like to hear a man relate narrative from his own experience. The late Russell E. Conwell delivered his lecture, "Acres of Diamonds", over six thousand times, and received millions for it.

Here are opening sentences taken from two stories that appeared in a single issue of *The Saturday Evening Post*:

1. "The sharp crack of a revolver punctuated the silence."
2. "An incident, trivial in itself but not at all trivial in its possible consequences, occurred at the Montview Hotel, Denver, during

the first week of July. It so aroused the curiosity of Goebel, the resident manager, that he referred it to Steve Faraday, owner of the Montview and half a dozen other Faraday hotels, when Steve made his regular visit a few days later on his midsummer swing of inspection."

Note that those openings have action. They start something. They arouse your curiosity. You want to read on, you want to know more, you want to find out what it is all about.

Even the unpractised beginner can usually manage a successful opening if he employs the story technique and arouses our curiosity.

BEGIN WITH A SPECIFIC ILLUSTRATION

It is difficult, it is arduous, for the average audience to follow abstract statements very long, Illustrations are easier to listen to, far easier. Then why not start with one? It is hard to get men to do that. I know. I have tried. They feel somehow that they must first make a few general statements. Not at all. Open with your Illustration, arouse then interest, then fellow with your general remarks.

What technique was employed to open this chapter you are now reading?

USE AN EXHIBIT

Perhaps the easiest way in the world to gain attention is to hold up something for people to look at. Even savages and halfwits, and babes in the cradle and monkeys in a zoo and dogs on the street will give heed to that kind of stimulus. It can be used sometimes with effectiveness before the most dignified audience. For example, Mr. S.S. Ellis opened one of his talks by holding a coin between his thumb and forefinger, and high above his shoulder. Naturally everyone looked. Then he inquired: "Has anyone here ever found a coin like this on the pavement? It announces that the fortunate finder will be given a lot free in such and such an estate development. He has but to call and present this coin...." Mr. Ellis then proceeded to reveal the coloured man in the cordwood and to condemn the misleading and unethical practices involved.

ASK A QUESTION

Mr. Ellis' opening has another commendable feature. It begins by asking a question, by getting the audience thinking with the speaker, cooperating with him. Note that the *Saturday Evening Post* article on gangsters opens with two questions in the first three sentences: "Are gangsters really organized?... How?" The use of this question-key is really one of the simplest, surest ways to unlock the minds of your audience and let yourself in. When other tools prove useless, you can always fall back on it.

WHY NOT OPEN WITH A QUESTION
FROM SOME FAMOUS MAN

The words of a prominent man always have attention power; so a suitable quotation is one of the very best ways of launching a harangue. Do you like the following opening of a discussion on business success?

"The world bestows its big prizes both in honours and money for but one thing," says Elbert Hubbard. "And that is initiative. And what is initiative? I'll tell you: it is doing the right thing without being told."

As a starter, that has several commendable features. The initial sentence arouses curiosity; it carries us forward, we want to hear more. If the speaker pauses skillfully after the words. "Elbert Hubbard," it arouses suspense. "What does the world bestow its big prizes for?" we ask. Quick. Tell us. We may not agree with you, but give us your opinion anyway... The second sentence leads up right into the heart of the subject. The third sentence, a question, invites the audience to get in on the discussion, to think, to do a little something. And how audiences like to do things. They love it! The fourth sentence defines initiative... After this opening, the speaker led off with a human interest story illustrating that quality. As far as construction is concerned. Moody might have rated the stock of that talk *Aaa*.

TIE YOUR TOPIC UP TO THE VITAL
INTERESTS OF YOUR HEARERS

Begin on some note that goes straight to the selfish interests of the audience. That is one of the best of all possible ways to start. It is sure to get attention. We are mightily interested in the things that touch us significantly, momentously.

That is only common sense, isn't it? Yet the use of it is very uncommon. For example, recently I heard a speaker begin a talk on the necessity of periodic health examinations. How did he open? By telling the history of the Life Extension Institute, how it was organized and the service it was rendering. Absurd! Our hearers have not the foggiest, not the remotest interest in how some company somewhere was formed, but they are stupendously and eternally interested in themselves.

Why not recognize that fundamental fact? Why not show how that company is of vital concern to them? Why not begin something like this? "Do you know how long you are expected to live according to life insurance tables? Your expectancy of life, as insurance statisticians phrase it, is two-thirds of the time between your present age and eighty. For example, if you are thirty-five now, the difference between your present age and eighty is forty-five; you can expect to live two-thirds of that amount, or another thirty years…. Is that enough? No, no, we are all passionately eager for more. Yet those tables are based upon millions of records. May you and I, then, hope to beat them? Yes, with proper precaution, we may; but the very first step is to have a thorough physical examination…."

Then, if we explain in detail why the periodic health examination is necessary, the hearer might be interested in some company formed to render that service. But to begin talking about the company in an impersonal way. It is disastrous! Deadly!

Take another example: During the last season. I heard a student begin a talk on the prime urgency of conserving our forests. He opened like this: "We ought to be proud of our national resources…" From that sentence, he went on to show that we were wasting our timber at a shameless and indefensible pace. But the opening was bad, too general, too vague. He did not make his subject seem vital to us. There was a printer in that audience. The destruction of our forests will mean something very real to his business. There was a banker; it is going to effect him for it will affect our general prosperity...and so on. Why not begin, then, by saying: "The subject I am going to speak about affects your business, Mr. Appleby; and yours, Mr. Saul. In fact, it will, in some measure, affect the price of the food we eat and the rent that we pay. It touches the welfare and prosperity of us all."

Is that exaggerating the importance of conserving our forests? No, I think not. It is only obeying Elbert Hubbard's injunction to "paint the picture large and put the matter in a way that compels attention".

THE ATTENTION POWER OF SHOCKING FACTS

"A good magazine article," said S.S. McClure, the founder of the periodical bearing his name, "is a series of shocks."

They jar us out of our daydreams; they seize, they demand attention. Here are some illustrations: Mr. N.D. Ballantine began his address on *The Marvels of Radio* with this statement: "Do you realize that the sound of a fly walking across a pane of glass here can be broadcasted by radio and made to roar away off in Central Africa like the falls of Niagara?"

Mr. Harry G. Jones, president of Harry G. Jones Company, began his talk on the *Criminal Situation* with these words: "'The administration of our criminal law,' declared William Howard Taft, then chief justice of the supreme court of the United States, 'is a disgrace to civilization.'"

That has the double advantage of being not only a shocking opening, but the shocking statement is quoted from an authority on jurisprudence.

Mr. Paul Gibbons, former President of the Optimist Club, opened an address on *crime* with these arresting statements: "The American people are the worst criminals in the world. Astounding as that assertion it, it is true, Cleveland, Ohio, has six times as many murders as all London. It has one hundred and seventy times as many robberies, according to its population, as has London. More people are robbed every year, or assaulted with intent to rob, in Cleveland than in all England, Scotland and Wales combined. More people are murdered every year in St. Louis than in all England and Wales. There are more murders in New York City than in all France or Germany or Italy or the British Isles. The sad truth of the matter is that the criminal in not punished. If you commit a murder, there is less than one chance in a hundred that you will ever be executed for it. You, as a peaceful citizen, are ten times as liable to die from cancer as you would be to be hanged if you shot a man."

That opening was successful, for Mr. Gibbons put the requisite power and earnestness behind his words. They lived. They breathed. However, I have heard other students begin their talks on the crime situation with somewhat similar illustrations; yet their openings were mediocre. Why? Words. Words. Words. Their technique of construction was flawless, but their spirit was nil. Their manner vitiated and emaciated all they said.

THE VALUE OF THE SEEMINGLY CASUAL OPENING

How do you like the following opening, and why? Mary E. Richmond is addressing the annual meeting of the League of Women Voters in the days before legislation against child marriages: Yesterday, as the train passed through a city not far away from here, I was reminded of a marriage that took place there a few years ago. Because many other marriages in this state have been just as hasty and disastrous as this one, I am going to begin what I have to say today with some of the details of this individual instance.

It was on December 12th that a high school girl of fifteen in that city met for the first time a junior in a nearby college who had just attained his majority. On December 15th, only three days later, they procured a marriage licence by swearing that the girl was eighteen and was therefore free from the necessity of procuring parental consent. Leaving the city clerk's office with their licence, they applied at once to a priest (the girl was a Catholic), but very properly he refused to marry them. In some way, perhaps through this priest, the child's mother received news of the attempted marriage. Before she could find her daughter, however, a justice of the peace had united the pair. The bridegroom then took his bride to a hotel where they spent two days and two nights, at the end of which time he abandoned her and never lived with her again.

Personally, I like that opening very much. The very first sentence is good. It forecasts and interesting reminiscence. We want to hear the details. We settle down to listen to a human interest story. In addition to that, it seems very natural. It does not smack of the study, it is not formal, it does not smell of the lamp.... "Yesterday, as the train passed through a city not far from here, I was reminded of a marriage that took place there a few years ago." Sounds natural, spontaneous, human. Sounds like one person relating an interesting story to another. An audience likes that. But it is very liable to shy at something too elaborate, something the reeks of preparation with malice aforethought. We want the art that conceals art.

> *"I've always been good at public speaking, but I never really enjoyed it. Then I started to really enjoy it, and that's made all the difference."*
>
> **—Mimi Kennedy**

> *"Before anything else, preparation is the key to success."*
>
> **—Alexander Graham Bell**

CHAPTER 3

....

How to Close a Talk

"Good speech: a beginning and a conclusion
placed not too far apart."

—Anonymous

Would you like to know in what parts of your speech are most likely to reveal your inexperience or your expertness, your inaptitude of your fitnesse? I'll tell you: in the opening and the closing. There is an old saying in the theatre, referring, of course, to actors, that goes like this: "By their entrances and their exits shall ye know them."

The beginning and the ending: They are the hardest things in almost any activity to manage adroitly. For example, at a social function aren't the most trying feats the graceful entrance and the graceful leave-taking? In a business interview, aren't the most difficult tasks the winning approach and the successful close?

The close is really the most strategic point in a speech; what one says last, the final words left ringing in the ears when one ceases—these are likely to be remembered longest. Beginners, however, seldom appreciate the importance of this coign of vantage. Their endings often leave much to be desired.

What are their most common errors? Let us discuss a few and search for remedies.

First, there is the man who finishes with: "That is about all I have to say on the matter; so I guess I shall stop. "That is not an ending. That is a mistake. That reeks of the amateur.

That is almost unpardonable. If that is all you have to say, why not round off your talk, and promptly take your seat and stop without talking about stopping. Do that, and the inference that that is all you have to say may, with safety and good taste, be left to the discernment of the audience.

Then there is the speaker who says all he has to say, but he does not know how to stop. I believe it was Josh Billings who advised people to take the bull by the tail instead of the horns, since it would be easier to let go. This speaker has the bull by the frontal extremities, and wants to part company with him, but try as hard as he will, he can't get near a friendly fence or tree. So he finally thrashes about in a circle, covering the same ground, repeating himself, leaving a bad impression....

The remedy? An ending has to be planned some time, doesn't it? Is it the part of wisdom to try to do it after you are facing an audience, while you are under the strain and stress of talking, while your mind must be intent on what you are saying? Or does common sense suggest the advisability of doing it quietly, calmly, beforehand?

Even such accomplished speakers as Webster. Bright, Gladstone, with their admirably command of the English language, felt it necessary to write down and all but memorize the exact words of their closings.

The beginner, if he follows in their footsteps, will seldom have cause to regret it. He ought to know very definitely with what ideas he is going to close. He ought to rehears the ending several times, using not necessarily the same phraseology during each repetition, but putting the thoughts definitely into words.

An extemporaneous talk, during the process of delivery, sometimes has to be altered vary materially; has to be cut and slashed to meet unforeseen developments, to harmonize with the reactions of one's hearers; so it is really wise to have two or three closings planned. If one does not fit, another way.

Some speakers never get to the end at all. Along in the middle of their journey, they begin to sputter and misfire like an engine when the petrol supply is about exhausted; after a few desperate lunges, they come to a complete standstill, a breakdown. They need, of course, better preparation, more practice—more petrol in the tank.

Many novices stop too abruptly. Their method of closing lacks smoothness, lacks finish. Properly speaking, they have no close; they merely cease suddenly, jerkily. The effect is unpleasant, amateurish. It is as if a friend in a social conversation were to break off brusquely and dart out of the room without a graceful leave-taking.

No less a speaker than Lincoln made that mistake in the original draft of his first inaugural. That speech was delivered at a tense time. The black storm clouds of dissension and hatred were already milling overhead. A few weeks later, the cyclone of blood and destruction burst upon the nation. Lincoln, addressing his closing words to the people of the South, had intended to end in this fashion:

> In your hands, my dissatisfied fellow-countrymen, and not in mine, is the momentous issue of the civil war. The government will not assail you. You can have no conflict without being yourselves the aggressors. You have no oath registered in heaven to destroy the government, while I have a most solemn one to preserve, protect and defend it. You can forbear the assault upon it. I cannot shrink from the defence of it. With you and not with me is the solemn question of "Shall it be peace or a sword?"

He submitted his speech to Secretary Seward. Seward quite appropriately pointed out that the ending was too blunt, too abrupt, too provocative. So Seward himself tried his hand at a closing; in fact, he wrote two. Lincoln accepted one of them and used it, with slight modifications, in place of the last three sentences of the close he had originally prepared. The result was that his First Inaugural Address now lost its provocative abruptness and rose to a climax of friendliness, of sheer beauty and poetical eloquence:

> I am loth to close. We are not enemies but friends. We must not be enemies. Though passion may have strained, it must not break our bonds of affection. The mystic chords of memory, stretching from every battlefield and patriot's grave to every living heart and

hearthstone all over this broad land, will swell the chorus of the Union when again touched, as surely they will be, by the better angel of our nature.

How can a beginner develop the proper *feeling* for the close of an address? By mechanical rules?

No. Like culture, it is too delicate for that. It must be a matter of sensing, almost of intuition. Unless a speaker can *feel* when it is done harmoniously, adroitly, how can he himself hope to do it?

However, this *feeling* can be cultivated; this expertness can be developed somewhat, by studying the ways in which accomplished speakers have achieved it. Here is an illustration, the close of an address by the then Prince of Wales before the Empire Club of Toronto:

> I am afraid, gentlemen, that I have departed from me reserve, and talked about myself a good deal too much. But I wanted to tell you, as the largest audience that I have been privileged to address in Canada, what I feel about my position and the responsibility which it entails. I can only assure you that I shall always endeavour to live up to that great responsibility and to be worthy of your trust.

A blind man listening to that talk would *feel* that it was ended. It isn't left dangling in the air like a loose rope. It isn't left ragged and jagged. It is rounded off, it is finished.

The famous Dr. Harry Emerson Fosdick spoke in the Geneva Cathedral of St. Pierre the Sunday after the opening of the sixth assembly of the League of Nations. He chose for his text: "All they that take the sword shall perish with the sword." Note the beautiful and lofty and powerful way in which he brought his sermon to a close:

> We cannot reconcile Jesus Christ and war—that is the essence of the matter. That is the challenge which today should stir the conscience of Christendom. War is the most colossal and ruinous social sin that afflicts mankind; it is utterly and irremediably unchristian; in its total method and effect it means everything

that Jesus did not mean and it means nothing that he did mean; it is a more blatant denial of every Christian doctrine about God and man than all the theoretical atheists on earth ever could devise. It would be worthwhile, would it not, to see the Christian Church claim as her own this greatest moral issue of our time, to see her lift once more as in our fathers' days, a clear standard against the paganism of this present world and, refusing to hold her conscience at the beck and call of belligerent states, put the kingdom of God above nationalism and call the world to peace? That would not be the denial of patriotism but its apotheosis.

Here today, as an American, under this high and hospitable roof, I cannot speak for my government, but both as an American and as a Christian I do speak for millions of my fellow citizens in wishing your great work, in which we believe, for which we pray, our absence from which we painfully regret, the eminent success which it deserves. We work in many ways for the same end—a world organized for peace. Never was an end better worth working for. The alternative is the most appalling catastrophe mankind has ever faced. Like gravitation in the physical realm, the law of the Lord in the moral realm bends for no man and no nation: "All they that take the sword shall perish with the sword."

But this collection of speech endings would not be complete without the majestic tones, the organ-like melody of the close of Lincoln's Second Inaugural. The late Earl Curzon of Keddleston, Chancellor of Oxford University, declared that this selection was "among the glories and treasures of mankind...the purest gold of human eloquence, nay, of eloquence almost divine":

Fondly do we hope, fervently do we pray, that this mighty scourge of war may speedily pass away. Yet if God wills that it continue until all the wealth piled by the bondsman's two hundred and fifty years of unrequited toil shall be sunk, and until every drop of blood drawn with the lash shall be paid by another drawn with the sword, as was said three thousand years ago, so still it must be said that 'the judgments of the Lord are true and righteous altogether'.

With malice toward none; with charity for all; with firmness in the right, as God gives us to see the right, let us strive on to finish the work we are in; to bind up the nation's wounds; to care for him who shall have borne the battle, and for his widow and his orphan—to do all which may achieve and cherish a just and lasting peace among ourselves, and with all nations.

You have just read, my dear reader, what is, in my opinion, the most beautiful speech ending ever delivered to the lips of mortal man… Do you agree with my estimate? Where, in all the range of speech literature, will you find more humanity, more sheer loveliness, more sympathy?

"Noble as was the Gettysburg Address," says William E. Barton in *Life of Abraham Lincoln,* "this rises to a still higher level of nobility… It is the greatest of the addresses of Abraham Lincoln and registers his intellectual and spiritual power at their highest altitude."

"This was like a sacred poem," wrote Carl Schurz. "No American President had ever spoken words like these to the American people. America had never had a president who had found such words in the depths of his heart."

But you are not going to deliver immortal pronouncements as President in Washington or as Prime Minister in Ottawa or Melbourne. Your problem, perhaps, will be how to close a simple talk before a group of businessmen. How shall you set about it? Let us search a bit. Let us see if we cannot uncover some fertile suggestions.

SUMMARIZE YOUR POINTS

Even in a short talk of three to five minutes, a speaker is very apt to cover so much ground that at the close the listeners are a little hazy about all his main points. However, few speakers realize that. They are misled into assuming that because these points are crystal clear in their own minds, they must be equally lucid to their hearers. Not at all. The speaker has been pondering over his ideas for some time. But his points are all new to the audience; they are flung at the audience like a handful of shot. Some may stick, but the most are liable to roll off in confusion. The hearers are liable, like Iago, to "remember a mass of things but nothing distinctly".

Some anonymous Irish politician is reported to have given this recipe for making a speech: "First, tell them that you are going to tell them, then tell them, then tell them that you have told them." Not bad, you know. In fact, it is often highly advisable to "tell them that you have told them". Briefly, of course, speedily—a mere outline, a summary.

Here is a good example. The speaker is a student of Mr. Bills, class in Public Speaking. He is also a traffic manager for railways:

> In short, gentlemen, our own backdoor yard experience with this block device, the experience in its use in the East, in the West, in the North—the sound operating principles underlying its operation, the actual demonstration in the money saved in one year in wreck prevention, move me most earnestly and unequivocally to recommend its immediate installation on our Southern branch.

You see what he has done? You can see it and feel it without having heard the rest of the talk. He has summed up in a few sentences, in sixty-two words, practically all the points he has made in the entire talk.

Don't you feel that a summary like that helps? If so, make that technique your own.

APPEAL FOR ACTION

The closing just quoted is an excellent illustration of the appeal-for-action ending. The speaker wanted something done: a block device installed on the Southern branch of his road. He based his appeal for it on the money it would save, on the wrecks it would prevent. The speaker wanted action, and he got it. This was not a mere practice talk. It was delivered before the board of directors of a certain railway, and it secured the installation of the block device for which it asked.

A TERSE, SINCERE COMPLIMENT

The great state of Pennsylvania should lead the way in hastening the coming of the new day. Pennsylvania, the great producer of iron and steel, mother of the greatest railroad company in the world, third among our agricultural states—Pennsylvania is the keystone of our business arch. Never was the prospect before her greater, never was her opportunity for leadership more brilliant.

With these words, Charles Schwab closed his address before the Pennsylvania Society of New York. He left his hearers pleased, happy, optimistic. That is an admirable way to finish; but, in order to be effective, it must be sincere. No gross flattery. No extravagances. This kind of closing, if it does not ring true, will ring false, very false. And like a false coin, people will have none of it.

A HUMOROUS CLOSE

"Always leave them laughing," said George Cohan, "when you say goodbye." If you have the ability to do it, and the material, fine! But how? That, as Hamlet said, is the question. Each man must do it his own individual way.

One would hardly expect Lloyd George to leave a gathering of Methodists laughing when he was talking to them on the ultra-solemn subject of John Wesley's Tomb, but note how cleverly he managed it. Note, also, how smoothly and beautifully the talk is rounded off:

I am glad you have taken in hand the repair of his tomb. It should be honoured. He was a man who had a special abhorrence of any absence of neatness or cleanliness. He it was, I think, who said, "Let no one ever see a ragged Methodist." It is due to him that you never can see one. (Laughter.) It is a double unkindness to leave his tomb ragged. You remember what he said to a Derbyshire girl who ran to the door as he was passing and cried, "God bless you, Mr. Wesley". "Young woman," he answered, "your blessing would be of more value if your face and apron were cleaner." (Laughter.) That was his feeling about untidiness. Do not leave his grave untidy. If he passed along, that would hurt him more than anything.

Do look after that. It is a memorable and sacred shrine. It is your trust. (Cheers.)

CLOSING WITH A POETICAL QUOTATION

Of all methods of ending, none are more acceptable, when well done, than humour or poetry. In fact, if you can get the proper verse of poetry for your closing. It is almost ideal. It will give the desired flavour. It will give dignity. It will give individuality. It will give beauty.

Rotarian Sir Harry Lauder closed his address to the Rotarian delegates at the Edinburgh convention in this fashion:

And when you get back home, some of you send me a postcard. I will send you one if you do not send me one. You will easily know it is from me because there will be no stamp on it. (Laughter.) But I will have some writing on it, and the writing will be this:

"Seasons may come and seasons may go,

Everything withers in due course, you know,

But there is one thing still blooms as fresh as the dew,

That is the love and affection I still have for you."

That little verse fits Harry Lauder's personality, and no doubt it fitted the whole tenor of his talk. Therefore, it was excellent for him. Had some formal and restrained Rotarian used it at the end of a solemn talk, it might have been so out of key as to be almost ridiculous. The longer I teach public speaking, the more clearly I see, the more vividly I feel, that it is impossible to give general rules that will serve on all occasions. So much depends upon the subject, the time, the place, and the man. Everyone must, as Saint Paul said, "work out his own salvation."

I was a guest recently at a farewell dinner given in honour of the departure of a certain professional man from New York City. A dozen speakers stood up in turn, eulogizing their departing friend, wishing him success in his new field of activity. A dozen talks, and only one ended in an unforgettable manner. That was one that closed with a poetical quotation. The speaker, with emotion in his voice, turned directly to the departing guest, crying: "And now, goodbye. Good luck. I wish you every good wish that you can wish yourself!"

> I touch my heart as the Easterns do:
> May the peace of Allah abide with you.
> Wherever you come, wherever you go,
> May the beautiful palms of Allah grow.
> Through days of labour and nights of rest,
> May the love of Allah make you blest.
> I touch my heart as the Easterns do:
> May the peace of Allah abide with you.

Mr. J.A. Abbott, Vice-President of the L.A.D. Motors Corporation of Brooklyn, spoke to the employees of his organization on the subject of Loyalty and Cooperation. He closed his address with this ringing verse from Kipling's *Second Jungle Book:*

> Now this is the Law of the jungle—as old and as true as the sky;
> And the Wolf that shall keep it may prosper, but the Wolf that shall break it must die.
> As the creeper that girdles the tree-trunk, the law runneth forward and back—
> For the strength of the Pack is the Wolf, and the strength of the Wolf is the Pack.

If you will go to the public library in your town and tell the librarian that you are preparing a talk on a certain subject and that you wish a poetical quotation to express this idea or that, she may be able to help you find something suitable in some reference volume such as Bartlett's book of quotations.

THE POWER OF A BIBLICAL QUOTATION

If you can quote a passage from Holy Writ to back up your speech, you are fortunate. A choice Biblical quotation often has a profound effect.

The well-known financier, Frank Vanderlip, used this method in ending his address on the Allied Debts to the United States:

> If we insist to the letter upon our claim, or claim will in all probability never be met. If we insists upon it selfishly, we realize in hatreds but not in cash. If we are generous, and wisely generous, those claims can all be paid, and the good we do with them will mean more to us materially than anything we would conceivably be parting with. "For whosoever will save his life shall lose it, but whosoever shall lose his life for my sake and the Gospel's, the same shall save it."

THE CLIMAX

The climax is a popular way of ending. It is often difficult to manage and is not an ending for all speakers not for all subjects. But when well done, it is excellent. It works up to a crest, a peak, getting stronger sentence by sentence.

Lincoln used the climax in preparing his notes for a lecture on Niagara Falls. Note how each comparison is stronger than the preceding, how he gets a cumulative effect by comparing its age to Columbus, Christ, Moses, Adam, and so on:

> It calls up the indefinite past. When Columbus first sought this continent—when Christ suffered on the cross—when Moses led Israel through the Red Sea—nay, even when Adam first came from the hands of his Maker; then, as now, Niagara was roaring here. The eyes of that species of extinct giants whose bones fill the mounds of America have gazed on Niagara, as ours do now. Contemporary with the first race of men, and older than the first man, Niagara is as strong and fresh today as ten thousand years ago. The Mammoth and Mastodon, so long dead that fragments of their monstrous bones alone testify that they ever lived, have gazed on Niagara—in that long, long time never still for a moment, never dried, never frozen, never slept, never rested.

Wendell Philips employed this selfsame technique in his address on Toussaint L'Ouverture. The close of it is quoted below. This selection is often cited in books on public speaking. It has vigour, vitality. It is interesting even though it is a bit too ornate for this practical age. This speech was written more than half a century ago. Amusing, isn't it, to note how woefully wrong were Wendell Philips' prognostications concerning the historical significance of John Brown and Toussaint L'Ouverture "fifty years hence when truth gets a hearing"? It is as hard evidently to guess history as it is to foretell next year's stock market or the price of lard.

I would call him Napoleon, but Napoleon made his way to empire over broken oaths and through a sea of blood. This man never broke his word. "No Retaliation" was his great motto and the rule of his life; and the last words uttered to his son in France were these: "My boy, you will one day go back to Santo Domingo; forget that France murdered your father." I would call him Cromwell, but Cromwell was only a soldier, and the state he founded went down with him into his grave. I would call him Washington, but the great Virginian held slaves. This man risked his empire rather than permit the slave-trade in the humblest village of his dominions.

You think me a fanatic tonight, for you read history, not with your eyes, but with your prejudices. But fifty years hence, when Truth gets a hearing, the Muse of History will put Phocion for the Greek, and Brutus for the Roman, Hampden for England, Lafayette for France, choose Washington as the bright, consummate flower of our earlier civilization, and John Brown the ripe fruit of our noonday, then, dipping her pen in the sunlight, will write in the clear blue, above them all, the name of the soldier, the statesman, the martyr, Toussaint L'Ouverture.

WHEN THE TOE TOUCHES

Hunt, search, experiment until you get a good ending and a good beginning. Then get them close together.

The speaker who does not cut his talk to fit in with the prevailing mood of this hurried, rapid age will be unwelcome and, sometimes, positively disliked.

No less a saint than Saul of Tarsus sinned in this respect. He preached until a chap in the audience, "a young man named Eutychus", went to sleep and fell out of a window and all but broke his neck. Even then he may not have stopped talking. Who knows? I remember a speaker, a doctor, standing up one night at a University Club. It had been a long banquet. Many speakers had already talked. It was two o'clock in the morning when his turn came. Had he been endowed with tact and fine feeling and discretion, he would have said half a dozen sentences and let us go home. But did he? No, not he. He launched into a forty-five minute tirade against vivisection. Long before he was halfway through his audience were wishing that he, like Eutychus, would fall out of a window and break something, anything, to silence him.

Mr. Lorimer, the editor of the *Saturday Evening Post,* told me that he always stopped a series of articles in the *Post* when they were at the height of their popularity, and people were clamouring for more. Why stop then? Why then of all times?

"Because," said Mr. Lorimer—and he ought to know—"the point of satiation is reached very soon after that peak of popularity."

The same wisdom will apply, and ought to be applied, to speaking. Stop while the audience is still eager to have you go on.

The greatest speech Christ ever delivered, the Sermon on the Mount, can be repeated in five minutes. Lincoln's Gettysburg address has only ten sentences. On can read the whole story of creation in Genesis in less time than it takes to peruse a murder story in the morning paper.... Be brief! Be brief!

Dr. Johnson, Archdeacon of Nyasa, has written a book about the primitive peoples of Africa. He has lived among them, observed them, for forty-nine years. He relates that when a speaker talks too long at a village gathering or the Gwang-wara, the audience silences him with shouts of "Imetosha! Imetosha!"—"Enough! Enough!"

Another tribe is said to permit a speaker to hold forth only so long as he can stand on one foot. When the toe of the lifted member touches the ground, *finito.* He has come to an end.

And the average white audience, even though they are more polite, more restrained, dislike long speeches as much as do those African negroes.

So be warned by their lot,

Which I know you will not,

And learn about speaking from them.

"*The conclusion, too, has definite work to perform, It rounds out the talk; it holds the audience's earnest attention for a brief moment on the speech as a whole.*"

—George Rowland Collins

"*Life is the art of drawing sufficient conclusions from insufficient premises.*"

—Samuel Butler

....

Self-Confidence through Preparation

*"One important key to success is self-confidence. An
important key to self-confidence is preparation."*

—Arthur Ashe

It has been my professional duty as well as pleasure to listen to and criticize approximately six thousand speeches a year each season since 1912.
These were made, not by college students, but by mature business and
professional men. If that experience has engraved on my mind any one
thing more deeply than another, surely it is this: the urgent necessity of
preparing a talk before one starts to make it and of having something
clear and definite to say, something that has impressed one, something
that won't stay unsaid. Aren't you unconsciously drawn to the speaker
who, you feel, has a real message in his head and heart that he zealously
desires to communicate to your head and heart? That is half the secret
of speaking.

When a speaker is in that kind of mental and emotional state he will
discover a significant fact: namely, that his talk will almost make itself. Its
yoke will be easy, its burden will be light. A well-prepared speech is already
nine-tenths delivered.

The primary reason why most men take this course, is to acquire
confidence and courage and self-reliance. And the one fatal mistake many
make is neglecting to prepare their talks. How can they even hope to
subdue the cohorts of fear, the cavalry of nervousness, when they go into
the battle with wet powder and blank shells, or with no ammunition at all?

Under the circumstances, small wonder that they are not exactly at home before an audience. "I believe," said Lincoln in the White House, "that I shall never be old enough to speak without embarrassment when I have nothing to say."

If you want confidence, why not do the things necessary to bring it about?

Why don't those enrolled in this course prepare their talks more carefully? Why? Some don't clearly understand what preparation is nor how to go about is wisely; others plead a lack of time. So we shall discuss these problems rather fully—and we trust lucidly and profitably—in this chapter.

THE RIGHT WAY TO PREPARE

What is preparation? Reading a book? That is one kind, but not the best. Reading may help; but if one attempts to lift a lot of "canned" thoughts out of a book and to give them out immediately as his own, the whole performance will be lacking in something. The audience may not know precisely what is lacking, but they will not warm to the speaker.

To illustrate: some time ago I conducted a course in public speaking for the senior officers of banks. Naturally, the members of such a group, having many demands upon their time, frequently found it difficult to prepare adequately or to do what they conceived of as preparing. All their lives they had been thinking their own individual thoughts, nurturing their own personal convictions, seeing things from their own distinctive angles, living their own original experiences. So, in that fashion they had spent forty years storing up material for speeches. But it was hard for some of them to realize that. They could not see the forest for "the murmuring pines and the hemlocks".

This group met Friday evenings from five to seven. One Friday, a certain gentleman connected with a bank—for our purposes here, we shall designate him as Mr. Jackson—found four-thirty had arrived, and, what was he to talk about? He walked out of his office, bought a copy of a magazine at a news stand and, in the subway coming down to the bank where the class met, he read an article entitled, "You Have Only Ten Years To Succeed". He read it not because he was interested in the article especially, but because he must speak on something, on anything, to fill his quote of time.

An hour later, he stood up and attempted to talk convincingly and interestingly on the contents of this article.

What was the result, the inevitable result?

He had not digested, had not assimilated what he was trying to say. "Trying to say"—that expresses it precisely. He was *trying*. There was no real message in him seeking for an outlet, and his whole manner and tone revealed it unmistakably. How could he expect the audience to be any more impressed than he himself was? He kept referring to the article saying the author said so and so. Their was a surfeit of the magazine in it, but regrettably little of Mr. Jackson.

So I addressed him somewhat in this fashion: "Mr. Jackson, we are not interested in this shadowy personality who wrote that article. He is not here. We can't see him. But we are interested in you and your ideas. Tell us what you think, personally, not what somebody else said. Put more of Mr. Jackson in this. Why not take this same subject for next week? Why not read this article again, and ask yourself whether you agree with the author or not? If you do, think out his suggestions and illustrate them with observations from your own experience. If you don't agree with him, say so and tell us why. Let this article be merely the starting point from which you launch your own speech."

Mr. Jackson accepted the suggestion, reread the article and concluded that he did not agree with the author at all. He did not sit down in the subway and try to prepare this next speech to order. He let it grow. It was a child of his own brain, and it developed and expanded and took on stature just as his physical children had done. And like his daughters, this other child grew day and night when he was least conscious of it. One thought was suggested to him while reading some item in the newspaper, another illustration swam into his mind unexpectedly when he was discussing the subject with a friend. The thing deepened and heightened, lengthened and thickened, as he thought over it during the odd moments of the week.

The next time Mr. Jackson spoke on this subject, he had something that was his, ore that he dug out of his own mine, currency coined in his own mint. And he spoke all the better because he was disagreeing with the author of the article. There is no spur to rouse one like a little opposition.

What an incredible contrast between these two speeches by the same man, in the same fortnight, on the same subject. What a colossal difference the right kind of preparation makes!

Let us cite another illustration of how to do it and how not to do it. A gentleman, whom we shall call Mr. Flynn, was a student of this course. One afternoon he devoted his talk to eulogizing his home tour. He had hastily and superficially gleaned his facts from a tourist booklet. They sounded like it—dry, disconnected, undigested. He had not thought over his subject adequately. It had not elicited his enthusiasm. He did not feel what he was saying deeply enough to make it worth while expressing. The whole affair was flat and flavourless and unprofitable.

A fortnight later something happened that touched Mr. Flynn to the core: a thief stole his motorcar out of a public garage. He rushed to the police and offered rewards, but it was all in vain. The police admitted that it was well nigh impossible for them to cope with the crime situation; yet, only a week previously, they had found time to walk about the street, chalk in hand, and fine Mr. Flynn because he had parked his car fifteen minutes at a kerb. These "chalk cops", who were so busy annoying respectable citizens that they could not catch criminals, aroused his ire. He was indignant. He had something now to say, not something that he had got out of a book but something that was leaping hot out of his own life and experience. Here was something that was part and parcel of the real man—something that had aroused his feelings and convictions. In his speech eulogizing the city, he had laboriously pulled out sentence by sentence; but now he had but to stand on his feet and open his mouth, and his condemnation of the police welled up and boiled forth like Vesuvius in action. A speech like that is almost foolproof. It can hardly fail. It was experience plus reflection.

WHAT IS MEANT BY PREPARATION

Does the preparation of a speech mean the getting together of some faultless phrases written down or memorized? No. Does it mean the assembling of a few casual thoughts that really convey very little to you personally? Not at all. It means the assembling of *your* thoughts, *your* ideas, your convictions *your* urges. And you have such thoughts, such urges. You have them every day of your waking life. They even swarm through your dreams. Your whole existence has been filled with feelings and experiences. These things are lying deep in your subconscious mind as thick as pebbles on the seashore. Preparation means thinking, brooding, recalling, selecting the ones that appeal to you most, polishing them, working them into a pattern, a mosaic of your own. That doesn't sound like such a difficult programme, does it? It isn't. It just requires a little concentration and thinking to a purpose.

THE SAGE ADVICE OF DEAN BROWN OF YALE

A few years ago the Yale Divinity School celebrated the one hundredth anniversary of its founding. On that occasion, the Dean, Dr. Charles Reynold Brown, delivered a series of lectures on the Art of Preaching. These are now published in book form under that name by the Macmillan Company, New York. Dr. Brown has been preparing addresses himself weekly for a third of a century, and also training others to prepare and deliver; so he was in a position to dispense some sage advice on the subject, advice that will hold good regardless of whether the speaker is a man of the cloth preparing a discourse on the Ninety-first Psalm, or a shoe manufacturer preparing a speech on Labour Unions. So I am taking the liberty of quoting Dr. Brown here:

Brood over your text and your topic. Brood over them until they become mellow and responsive. You will hatch out of them a whole flock of promising ideas hatch out of them a whole flock of promising ideas as you cause the tiny germs of life there contained to expand and develop....

It will be all the better if this process can go on for a long time and not be postponed until Saturday afternoon when you are actually making you final preparation for Sunday. If a minister can hold a certain truth in his mind for a month, for six months perhaps, for a year it may be before he preaches on it he will find new ideas perpetually sprouting out of it, until it shows and abundant growth. He may meditate on it as he walks the streets, or as he spends some hours on a train, when his eyes are too tired to read.

He may indeed brood upon it in the night-time. It is better for the minister not to take his church or his sermon to bed with him habitually—a pulpit is a splendid thing to preach from, but it is not a good bedfellow. Yet, for all that, I have sometimes got out of bed in the middle of the night to put down the thoughts which came to me, for fear I might forget them before morning...

When you are actually engaged in assembling the material for a particular sermon, write down everything that comes to you bearing upon that text and topic. Write down what you saw in the text when you first chose it. Write down all the associated ideas which now occur to you...

Put all these ideas of yours down in writing, just a few words, enough to fix the idea, and keep your mind reaching for more all the time as if it were never to see another book as long as it lived. This is the way to train the mind in productiveness. You will by this method keep your own mental processes fresh, original, creative...

Put down all of those ideas which you have brought to the birth yourself, unaided. They are more precious for your mental unfolding than rubies and diamonds and much fine gold. Put them down, preferably on scraps of paper, backs of old letters, fragments of envelopes, waste paper, anything which comes to your hand. This is much better in every way than to use nice, long, clean sheets of foolscap. It is not a mere matter of economy—you will find it easier to arrange and organize these loose bits when you come to set your material in order.

Keep on putting down all the ideas which come to your mind, thinking hard all the while. You need not hurry this process. It is one of the most important mental transactions in which you will be privileged to engage. It is this method which causes the mind to grow in real productive power....

You will find that the sermons you enjoy preaching the most and ones which actually accomplish the most good in the lives of your people will be those sermons which you take most largely out of your own interiors. They are bone of your bone, flesh of your flesh, the children of your own mental labour, the output of your own creative energy. The sermons which are garbled and compiled will always have a kind of second-hand, warmed-over flavour about them. The sermons which live and move and enter into the temple, walking and leaping and praising God, the sermons which enter into the hearts of men causing them to mount up with wings like eagles and to walk in the way of duty and not faint—these real sermons are the ones which are actually born from the vital energies of the man who utters them.

HOW LINCOLN PREPARED HIS SPEECHES

How did Lincoln prepare his speeches? Fortunately, we know the facts and, as you read here of his method, you will observe that Dean Brown, in his lecture, commended several of the procedures that Lincoln had employed three-quarters of a century previously. One of Lincoln's most famous addresses was that in which he declared with prophetic vision: "A house divided against itself cannot stand.' I believe this government cannot endure, permanently, half-slave and half-free." This speech was thought out as he went about his usual work, as he ate his meals, as he walked the street, as he sat in his barn milking his cow, as he made his daily trip to the butcher shop and grocery, and old grey shawl over his shoulders, his market basket over his arm, his little son at his side, chattering and questioning, growing peeved, and jerking at the long bony fingers in a vain effort to make his father talk to him. But Lincoln stalked on, absorbed in his own reflections, thinking of his speech, apparently unconscious of the boy's existence.

From time to time during this brooding and hatching process, he jotted down notes, fragments, sentences here and there on stray envelopes, scraps of paper, bits torn from paper sacks—anything that was near. These he stowed away in the top of his hat and carried them there until he was ready to sit down and arrange them in order, and to write and revise the whole thing, and to shape it up for delivery and publication.

In the joint debates of 1858, Senator Douglas delivered the same speech wherever he went; but Lincoln kept studying and contemplating and reflecting until he found it easier, he said, to make a new speech each day than to repeat and old one. The subject was for ever widening and enlarging in his mind.

A short time before he moved into the White House, he took a copy of the Constitution and three speeches, and with only these for reference, he locked himself in a dingy, dusty back room over a store in Springfield; and there, away from all intrusion and interruption, he wrote out his inaugural address.

How did Lincoln prepare his Gettysburg address? Unfortunately, false reports have been circulated about it. The true story, however, is fascinating. Let us have it:

When the commission in charge of the Gettysburg cemetery decided to arrange for a formal dedication, they invited Edward Everett to deliver the speech. He had been a Boston minister, President of Harvard, Governor of Massachusetts, United States Senator, Minister to England, Secretary of State, and was generally considered to be America's most capable speaker. The date first set for the dedication ceremonies was October 23, 1863. Mr. Everett very wisely declared that it would be impossible for him to prepare adequately on such short notice. So the dedication was postponed until November 19, nearly a month, to give him to prepare. The last three days of that period he spent in Gettysburg, going over the battlefield, familiarizing himself with all that had taken place there. That period of brooding and thinking was most excellent preparation. It made the battle real to him.

Invitations to be present were despatched to all the members of Congress, to the President and his cabinet. Most of these declined; the committee was surprised when Lincoln agreed to come. Should they ask him to speak? They had not intended to do so. Objections were raised. He would not have time to prepare. Besides, even if he did have time, had he the ability? True, he could handle himself well in a debate on slavery; but no one had ever heard him deliver a dedicatory address. This was a grave and solemn occasion. They ought not to take any chances. Should they ask him to speak? They wondered, wondered.... But they would have wondered a thousand times more had they been able to look into the future and to see that this man, whose ability they were questioning, was to deliver on that occasion what is very generally accepted now as one of the most enduring addresses ever delivered by the lips of mortal man.

Finally, a fortnight before the event, they sent Lincoln a belated invitation to make "a few appropriate remarks". Yes, that is the way they worded it: "a few appropriate remarks". Think of writing that to the President of the United States!

Lincoln immediately set about preparing. He wrote to Edward Everett, secured a copy of the address that that classic scholar was to deliver and, a day or two later, going to a photographer's gallery to pose for his photograph, Lincoln took Everett's manuscript with him and read it during the spare time that he had at the studio. He thought over his talk for days, thought over it while walking back and forth between the White House and the War Office, thought over it while he stretched out on a leather couch in the War Office waiting for the late telegraphic reports. He wrote a rough draft of it on a piece of foolscap paper, and carried it about in the top of his tall silk hat. Ceaselessly he was brooding over it, ceaselessly it was taking shape. The Sunday before it was delivered he said to Noah Brooks: "It is not exactly written. It is not finished anyway. I have written it over two or three times, and I shall have to give it another lick before I am satisfied."

He arrived in Gettysburg the night before the dedication. The little town was filled to overflowing. Its usual population of thirteen hundred had suddenly swelled to fifteen thousand. The pavements became clogged, impassable, men and women took to the dirt streets. Half a dozen bands were playing; crowds were singing "John Brown's Body". People foregathered before the home of Mr. Wills where Lincoln was being entertained. They serenaded him; they demanded a speech. Lincoln responded with a few words which conveyed with more clearness than tact, perhaps, that he was unwilling to speak until the morrow. The facts are that he was spending the latter part of that evening giving his speech "another lick". He even went to an adjoining house where Secretary Seward was staying and read the speech aloud to him for his criticism. After breakfast the next morning, he continued "to give it another lick", working on it until a rap came at the door informing him that it was time for him to take his place in the procession. "Colonel Carr, who rode just behind the President, stated that when the procession started, the President sat erect on his horse, and looked the part of the commander-in-chief of the army; but, as the procession moved on, his body leaned forward, his arms hung limp, and his head was bowed, he seemed absorbed in thought."

We can only guess that even then he was going over his little speech of ten immortal sentences, giving it "another lick".

Some of Lincoln's speeches, in which he had only a superficial interest, were unquestioned failures, but he was possessed of extraordinary power when he spoke of slavery and the union. Why? Because he thought ceaselessly on these problems and felt deeply. A companion who shared a room with him one night in an Illinois tavern awoke next morning at daylight to find Lincoln sitting up in bed, staring at the wall, and his first words were: "This government cannot endure permanently half-slave and half-free."

How did Christ prepare His addresses? He withdrew from the crowd. He thought. He brooded. He pondered. He went out alone into the wilderness and meditated and fasted for forty days and forty nights. From that time on," records Saint Matthew, "Jesus began to preach." Shortly after that, He delivered one of the world's most celebrated speeches: the Sermon on the Mount.

"That is all very interesting," you may protest, "but I have no desire to become an immortal orator. I merely want to make a few simple talks in business occasionally."

True, and we realize your wants fully. This course is for the specific purpose of helping you and other businessmen like you to do just that. But, unpretending as the talks of yours may prove to be, you can profit by and utilize in some measure the methods of the famous speakers of the past.

HOW TO PREPARE YOUR TALK

What topics ought you to speak on during the sessions of this course? Anything that interests you. If possible, choose your own topics; you will be more fortunate still if your topic chooses you. However, you will often have topics suggested for you by your instructor.

Don't make the almost universal mistake of trying to cover too much ground in a brief talk. Just take one or two angles of a subject and attempt to cover them adequately. You will be fortunate if you can do that in the short speeches that are necessitated by the time schedule of this course.

Determine your subject a week in advance so that you will have time to think it over in odd moments. Think it over for seven days; dream over it for seven nights. Think of it the last thing when you retire. Think of it the next morning while you are shaving, while you are bathing, while you are riding downtown, while you are waiting for lifts, for lunch, for appointments. Discuss it with your friends. Make it a topic of conversation.

Ask yourself all possible questions concerning it. If, for example, you are to speak on divorce, ask yourself what causes divorce, what are the effects economically, socially. How can the evil be remedied? Should divorce be made impossible? More difficult? Easier?

Suppose you were going to talk on why you enrolled for this course. You ought then to ask yourself such questions as these: What are my troubles? What do I hope to get out of this instruction? Have I ever made a public talk? If so, when? Where? What happened? Why do I think this training is valuable for businessman? Do I know men who are forging ahead commercially largely because of their self-confidence, their presence, their ability to talk convincingly? Do I know others who will probably never achieve a gratifying measure of success because they lack these positive assets? Be specific. Tell the stories of these men without mentioning their names.

If you stand up think clearly and keep going for two or three minutes, that is all that will be expected of you during your first few talks. A topic, such as why you enrolled for this course, is very easy; that is obvious. If you will spend a little time selecting and arranging your material on that topic, you will be almost sure to remember it, for you will be speaking of your own observations, your own desires, your own experiences.

On the other hand, let us suppose that you have decided to speak on your business or profession. How shall you set about preparing such a talk? You already have a wealth of material on that subject. Your problem, then, will be to select and arrange it. Do not attempt to tell us all about it in three minutes. It can't be done. The attempt will be too sketchy, to fragmentary. Take one and only one phase of your topic: expand and enlarge that. For example, why not tell us how you came to be in your particular business

or profession? Was it a result of accident or choice? Relate your early struggles, your defeats, your hopes, your triumphs. Give us a human interest
narrative, a real life picture based on first-hand experiences. The truthful,
inside story of almost any man's life—if told modestly and without offending
egotism—is most entertaining. It is almost sure-fire speech material.

Or take another angle of your business: What are its troubles? What
advice would you give to a young man entering it?

Or tell us about the people with whom you come in contact—the
honest and dishonest onces. Tell us of your problems with labour, your
problems with your customers. What has your business taught you about
the most interesting topic in the world: human nature? If you speak about
the technical side of your business, about things, your talk may very easily
prove uninteresting to others. But people, personalities—one can hardly
go wrong with that kind of material.

Above all else, don't make your talk an abstract preachment. That will
bore us. Make your talk a regular layer cake of illustrations and general
statements. Think of concrete cases you have observed, and of the fundamental truths which you believe those specific instances illustrate. You
will also discover that these concrete cases are far easier to remember
than abstractions; they are far easier to talk about. They will also aid and
brighten your delivery.

Some men, in speaking of their businesses, commit the unforgiv-
able error of talking only of the features that interest them. Shouldn't the
speaker try to ascertain what will entertain not himself but his hearers?
Shouldn't he try to appeal to their selfish interests? If, for example, he sells
fire insurance, shouldn't he tell them how to prevent fires on their own
property? If he is a banker, shouldn't he give them advice on finance or
investments?

While preparing, study your audience. Think of their wants, their
wishes. That is sometimes half the battle.

In preparing some topics, it is very advisable—if time permits—to do
some reading, to discover what others have thought, what others have said
on the same subject. But don't read until you have first thought yourself
dry. That is important—very. Then go to the public library and lay your
needs before the librarian. Tell her you are preparing a speech on such and

state a topic. Ask her frankly for help. If you are not in the habit of doing research work, you will probably be surprised at the aids she can put at your disposal; perhaps a special volume on your very topic, outlines and briefs for debate, giving the principal arguments on both sides of the public questions of the day, the *Reader's Guide to Periodical Literature* listing the magazine articles that have appeared on various topics since the beginning of the century, the *Daily Mail Almanac,* the Encyclopæ-dias, and dozens of reference books. They are tools in your workshop. Use them.

THE SECRET OF RESERVE POWER

A Speech ought to be prepared somewhat in a lavish and discriminating spirit. Assemble a hundred thoughts, and discard ninety.

Collect more material, more information, than there is any possibility of employing. Get it for the additional confidence it will give you, for the sureness of touch. Get it for the effect it will have on your mind and heart and whole manner of speaking. This is a basic, important factor of preparation; yet it is constantly ignored by speakers, both in public and private.

"I have drilled hundreds of salesmen, canvassers, and demonstrators," says Arthur Dunn, "and the principal weakness which I have discovered in most of them has been their failure to realize the importance of knowing everything possible about their products and getting such knowledge before they start to sell.

Many salesmen have come to my office and after getting a description of the article and a line of sales talk have been eager to get right out and try to sell. Many of these salesmen have not lasted a week and a large number have not lasted forty-eight hours. In educating and drilling canvassers and salesmen in the sale of a food specialty, I have endeavoured to make food experts of them. I have compelled them to study food charts issued by the Department of Agriculture, which show in food the amount of water, the amount of protein, the amount of carbohydrates, the amount of fat, and ash. I have had them study the elements which make up the products which they are to sell. I have had them go to school for several days and then pass examinations. I have had them sell the product to other salesmen. I have offered prizes for the best sales talks.

I have often found salesmen who get impatient at preliminary time required for the study of their articles. They have said, "I will never have time to tell all of this to a retail grocer. He is too busy. If I talk protein and carbohydrates, he won't listen and, if he does listen, he won't know what I am talking about." My reply has been, "You don't get all of this knowledge for the benefit of your customer, but for the benefit of yourself. If you know your product from A to Z you will have a feeling about it that is difficult to describe. You will be so positively charged, so fortified, so strengthened in your own mental attitude that you will be both irresistible and unconquerable."

Miss Ida M. Tarbell, the well-known historian of the Standard Oil Company, told the writer that years ago, when she was in Paris, Mr. S.S. McClure, the founder of McClure's Magazine, cabled her to write a short article about the Atlantic Cable. She went to London, interviewed the European manager of the principal cable, and obtained sufficient data for her assignment. But she did not stop there. She wanted a reserve supply of facts, so she studied all manner of cables on display in the British Museum, she read books on the history of the cable and even went to manufacturing concerns on the edge of London and saw cables in the process of construction.

Why did she collect ten times as much information as she could possible use? She did it because she felt it would give her reserve power; because she realized that the things she knew and did not express would lend force and colour to the little she did express.

Edwin James Cattell has spoken to approximately thirty million people, yet he confided to me recently that if he did not, on the way home, kick himself for the good things he had left out of his talk, he felt that the performance must have been a failure. Why? Because he knew from long experience that the talks of distinct merit are those in which there abounds a reserve of material, a plethora, a profusion of it—far more than the speaker has time to use.

"What!" you object. "Does this author imagine that I can find time for all this? I would like him to know that I have a business to conduct and a wife and two children and a couple of Airedale dogs to support.... I can't be running to museums and looking at cables and reading books and sitting up in bed at daylight mumbling my speeches."

My dear sir, we know all about your case, and sympathetic allowance has been made for it. The assigned topics will be questions on which you have already done considerable thinking. Sometimes you will not be asked to plan any kind of a speech in advance, but you will be given an easy topic for impromptu speaking after you face your audience. This will afford you most useful practice in thinking on your feet—the sort of thing that you may be forced to do in business discussions.

Some of the men who join this course are only slightly interested in learning to prepare talks in advance. They want to be able to think on their feet and to join in discussions that come up at various business meetings. Such students sometimes prefer to come to the class, listen, and then take their cue from some of the preceding speakers. A limited amount of this may be advisable, but don't overdo it. Follow the suggestions given in this chapter. They will give you the ease and freedom you are seeking and also the ability to prepare talks effectively.

If you procrastinate until you have leisure to prepare and plan your talk, the leisure will probably never be found. However, it is easy to do the habitual, the accustomed thing, isn't it? So why not set aside one specific evening a week, from eight to ten o'clock, to be devoted to nothing but this task? That is the sure way, the systematic way. Why not try it?

"There is only security, and when you've lost that security, you've lost everything you've got. And that is the security of confidence in yourself; to be, to create, to make any position you want to make for yourself. And when you lose that confidence, you've lost the only security you can have... Self-confidence is self-determinism. One's belief in one's ability to determine his own course. As long as one has that, he's got the universe in his pocket. And when he hasn't got that, not all the pearls in China nor all the grain and corn in Iowa can give him security, because that's the only security there is."

—L. Ron Hubbard

CHAPTER 5

....

How Famous Speakers Prepared Their Addresses

"Luck is what happens when preparation meets opportunity."

—Seneca

I was present once at a luncheon of a Rotary Club when the principle speaker was a prominent government official. The high position that he occupied gave him prestige, and we were looking forward with pleasure to hearing him. He had promised to tell us about the activities of his own department, and it was one in which almost every businessman was interested.

He knew his subject thoroughly, knew far more about it then he could possibly use, but he had not planned his speech. He had not selected his material. He had not arranged it in orderly fashion. Nevertheless, with a courage born in inexperience, he plunged heedlessly, blindly, into his speech. He did not know where he was going, but he was on his way.

His mind was, in short, a mere hodgepodge, and so was the mental feats he served us. He brought on the ice cream first, and then placed the soup before us. Fish and nuts came next. And, on top of that, there was something that seemed to be a mixture of soup and ice cream and good red herring. I have never, anywhere or at any time, seen a speaker more utterly confused.

He had been trying to talk impromptu, but, in desperation now, he drew a bundle of notes out of his pocket, confessing that his secretary had

compiled them for him—and no one questioned the veracity of his assertion. The notes themselves evidently had no more order than a van full of
scrap iron. He fumbled through them nervously, glancing from one page
to another, trying to orient himself, trying to find a way out of the wilderness, and he attempted to talk as he did so. It was impossible. He apolo-
gized and, calling for water, took a drink with a trembling hand, uttered
a few more scattering sentences, repeated himself, dug into his notes
again…. Minute by minute he grew more helpless, more lost, more bewil-
dered, more embarrassed. Nervous perspiration stood out on his forehead,
and his handkerchief shook as he wiped it away. We in the audience sat
watching the fiasco, our sympathies stirred, our feelings harrowed. We
suffered positive and vicarious embarrassment. But with more doggedness
than discretion, the speaker continued, floundering, studying his notes,
apologizing and drinking. Everyone expect him felt that the spectacle was
rapidly approaching total disaster, and it was a relief to us all when he sat
down and ceased his death struggles. It was one of the most uncomfortable
audiences I have ever been in, and he was the most ashamed and humiliated speaker I have ever seen. He had made his talk as Rousseau said a
love letter should be written: he had begun without knowing what he was
going to say, and he had finished without knowing what he had uttered.

The moral of the tale is just this: "When a man's knowledge is not in
order," said Herbert Spencer, "the more of it he has, the greater will be his
confusion of thoughts."

No sane man would start to build a house without some sort of plan,
but why will he begin to deliver a speech without the vaguest kind of
outline or programme?

A speech is a voyage with a purpose, and it must be charted. The man
who starts nowhere, generally gets there.

I wish that I could paint this saying of Napoleon's in flaming letters of
red a foot high over every doorway on the globe where students of public
speaking foregather: "The art of war is a science in which nothing succeeds
which has not been calculated and thought out."

That is just as true of speaking as of shooting. But do speakers realize it,
or, if they do, do they always act on it? They do not. Most emphatically

they do not. Many a talk has just a trifle more plan and arrangement than a bowl of Irish stew.

What is the best and most effective arrangement for a given set of ideas? No one can say until he has studied them. It is always a new problem, an eternal question that every speaker must ask and answer himself again and again. No infallible rules can be given, but we can, at any rate, illustrate briefly here with a concrete case just what we mean by orderly arrangements.

HOW A PRIZE WINNING SPEECH WAS CONSTRUCTED

Here is a speech that was delivered by a student of this course before the Thirteenth Annual Convention of the American National Association of Real Estate Boards. It won first prize in competition with twenty-seven other speeches on various cities. This speech is well constructed, full of facts stated clearly, vividly, interestingly. It has spirit. It marches. It will merit reading and study.

Mr. Chairman and Friends:

Back 144 years ago, this great nation, the United States of America, was born in my City of Philadelphia, and so it is quite natural that a city having such a historical record should have that strong American spirit that has not only made it the greatest industrial centre in this country, but also one of the largest and most beautiful cities in the whole world.

Philadelphia has a population close to two millions of people, and our city has an area that is equal to the combined size of Milwaukee and Boston, Paris and Berlin, and out of our 130 square miles of territory we have given up nearly 8,000 acres of our best land for beautiful parks, squares and boulevards, so that our people would have the proper places for recreation and pleasure, and the right kind of environment that belongs to every decent American.

Philadelphia, friends, is not only a large, clean and beautiful city, but it is also known everywhere as the great workshop of the world, and the reason it is called the workshop of the world is because we have a vast army of ever 400,000 people employed in 9,200 industrial establishments that turn out one hundred thousand dollars' worth of useful commodities every ten minutes of the working day, and, according to a well-known statistician, there is no city in this country that equals Philadelphia in the production of woollen goods, leather goods, knit goods, textiles, felt hats, hardware, tools, storage batteries, steel ships and a great many other things. We build a railroad locomotive every two hours day and night, and more than one-half the people in this great country ride street cars made in the City of Philadelphia. We manufacture a thousand cigars every minute, and last year, in our 115 hosiery mills, we made two pairs of stockings for every man, woman and child in this country. We make more carpets and rugs than all of Great Britain and Ireland combined, and, in fact, our total commercial and industrial business is so stupendous that our bank clearings last year, amounting to thirty-seven billions of dollars, would have paid for every Liberty Bond in the entire country.

But, friends, while we are very proud of our wonderful industrial progress, and while we are also very proud of being one of the largest medical, art and educational centres in this country, yet, we feel a still greater pride in the fact that we have more individual homes in the City of Philadelphia than there are in any other city in the whole world. In Philadelphia we have 397,000 separate homes, and if these homes were placed on twenty-five-foot lots, side by side, in one single row, that row would reach all the way from Philadelphia clear through to this Convention Hall, at Kansas City, and then on to Denver, a distance of 1,881 miles.

But, what I want to call your special attention to, is the significance of the fact, that tens of thousands of these homes are owned and occupied by the working people of our city, and when a man owns the ground upon which he stands and the roof over his head, there is no argument ever presented that would infect that man with those imported diseases, known as Socialism and Communism.

Philadelphia is not a fertile soil for anarchy, because our homes, our educational institutions, and our gigantic industry have been produced by that true American spirit that was born in our city, and is a heritage from our forefathers. Philadelphia is the mother city of this great country, and the very fountainhead of American liberty. It is the city where the first American flag was made; it is the city where the First Congress of the United States met; it is the city where the Declaration of Independence was signed; it is the city where that best loved relic in America, the Liberty Bell, has inspired tens of thousands of our men, women and children, so that we believe we have a sacred mission, which is not to worship the golden calf, but to spread the American spirit, and to keep the fires of freedom burning, so that with God's permission, the Government of Washington, Lincoln and Roosevelt may be an inspiration to all humanity.

In the first place, this speech has a beginning and an ending. That is a rare virtue, my dear reader, more rare than you may be inclined to think. It starts somewhere. It goes there straight as wild geese on the wing. It doesn't dawdle. It loses no time.

It has freshness, individuality. The speaker opens by saying something about his city that the other speakers could not possible say about theirs: he points out that his city is the birthplace of the entire nation.

He states that it is one of the largest and most beautiful cities in the world. But that claim is general, trite; standing by itself, it would not impress anyone very much. The speaker knew that, so he helped his audience visualize the magnitude of Philadelphia by stating it "has an area equal to the combined size of Milwaukee, Boston, Paris and Berlin." That is definite, concrete. It is interesting. It is surprising. It makes a mark. It drives home the idea better than a whole page of statistics would have done.

Next he declares that Philadelphia is "known everywhere as the great workshop of the world". Sounds exaggerated, doesn't it? Like propaganda. Had he proceeded immediately to the next point no one would have been convinced. But he doesn't. He pauses to enumerate the products in which Philadelphia leads the world: "Woollen goods, leather goods, knit goods, textiles, felt hats, hardware, tools, storage batteries, steel ships." Doesn't sound so much like propaganda now, does it? Philadelphia "builds a railroad locomotive every two hours day and night, and more than one-half the people in this great country ride in street cars made in the city of Philadelphia".

"Well, I never knew that," we muse. "Perhaps I rode downtown yesterday in one of those street cars. I'll look tomorrow and see where my town buys its cars."

"A thousand cigars every minute...two pairs of stockings for every man, woman and child in this country."

We are still more impressed.... "Maybe my favourite cigar is made in Philadelphia...and these socks I have on..."

What does the speaker do next? Jump back to the subject of the size of Philadelphia that he covered first and give us some fact that he forgot then? No, not at all. He sticks to a point until he finishes it, has done with it, and need never return to it again. For that we are duly grateful, Mr. Speaker. For what is more confusing and muddling than to have a speaker darting from one tiling to another and back again as erratic as a bat in the twilight? Yet many a speaker does just that. Instead of covering his points in order, 1, 2, 3, 4, 5, he covers them as a football captain calls out signals—27, 34, 19, 2. No, he is worse than that. He covers them like this—27, 34, 27, 19, 2, 34, 19.

But this speaker, however, steams straight ahead on schedule time, never idling, never turning back, swerving neither to the right nor left, like one of those locomotives he has been talking about.

But he makes now the weakest point of his entire speech: Philadelphia, he declares, is "one of the largest medical, art and educational centres in this countrys". He merely announces that, then speeds on to something else—only twelve words to animate that fact, to make it vivid, to engrave it on the memory. Only twelve words lost, submerged, in a sentence containing a total of sixty-five. It doesn't work. Of course not. The human mind does not operate like a string of steel traps. He devotes so little time to this point, is so general, so vague, seems so unimpressed himself, that the effect on the hearer is almost nil. What should he have done? He realized that he could establish this point with the selfsame technique that he just employed to establish the fact that Philadelphia is the workshop of the world. He knew that. He also knew that he would have a stopwatch held on him during the contest, that he would have five minutes, not a second more; so he had to slur over this point or slight others.

There are "more individual homes in the city of Philadelphia than there are in any other city in the world". How does he make this phase of his topic impressive and convincing? First, he gives the number: 397,000. Second, he visualizes the number: "if these homes were placed on twenty-five foot lots, side by side, in one single row, that row would reach all the way from Philadelphia clear through this Convention Hall at Kansas City, and then on to Denver, a distance of 1,881 miles."

His audience probably forgot the number he gave before he had finished the sentence. But forget that picture? That would have been well nigh impossible.

So much for cold material facts. But they are not the stuff out of which eloquence is fashioned. This speaker aspired to build up to a climax, to touch the heart, to stir the feelings. So now on the home stretch, he deals with emotional material. He tells what the ownership of those homes means to the spirit of the city. He denounced "those imported diseases, known as Socialism and Communism…anarchy". He eulogizes Philadelphia as "the very fountainhead of American liberty". Liberty! A magic word, a word full of feeling, a sentiment for which millions have laid down their lives. That phrase it itself is good, but it is a thousand times better when he backs it up with concrete references to historic events and documents, dear, sacred, to the hearts of his hearers…. "It is the city where the first American Flag was made; it is the city where first Congress of the United States met; it is the city where the Declaration of Independence was signed…Liberty Bell…a sacred mission…to spread the American spirit…to keep the fires of freedom burning, so that with God's permission, the Government of Washington, Lincoln and Roosevelt may be an inspiration to all humanity." That is a real climax!

So much for the composition of this talk. But admirable as it is from the standpoint of construction, this speech could have come to grief, could easily have been brought to naught, had it been expressed in a calm manner devoid of all spirit and vitality. But the speaker delivered it as he composed it; with a feeling and enthusiasm born of the deepest sincerity. Small wonder that it won first prize, that it was awarded the Chicago Cup.

THE WAY DOCTOR CONWELL PLANNED HIS SPEECHES

There are not, as I have already said, any infallible rules that will solve the question of the best arrangement. There are no designs or schemes or charts that will fit all or even a majority of speeches; yet here are a few speech plans that will prove usable in some instances. The late Dr. Russell H. Conwell, the author of the famous *Acres of Diamonds*—once informed me that he had built many of his innumerable speeches on this outline:

1. State your facts.
2. Argue from them.
3. Appeal for action.

Many students of this course have found this plan very helpful and stimulating.

1. Show something that is wrong.
2. Show how to remedy it.
3. Ask for cooperation.

Or to put it in another way:

1. Here is a situation that ought to be remedied.
2. We ought to do so and so about the matter.
3. You ought to help for these reasons.

Yet another speech plan could be:

1. Secure interested attention.
2. Win confidence.
3. State your facts; educate people regarding the merits of your proposition.
4. Appeal to the motives that make men act.

SECRETS OF GREAT SPEAKERS

Woodrow Wilson

"I begin," said Woodrow Wilson when asked to explain his methods, "with a list of the topics I want to cover *arranging them in my mind in their natural relations*—that is, I fit the bones of the thing together; then I write it out in shorthand. I have always been accustomed to writing in shorthand, finding it a great saver of time. This done, I copy it on my own typewriter, changing phrases, correcting sentences, and adding material as I go along."

Theodore Roosevelt

Theodore Roosevelt prepared his talks in the characteristic Rooseveltian manner: he dug all the facts, reviewed them, appraised them, determined their findings, arrived at his conclusions, arrived with a feeling of certainty that was unshakable.

Then, with a pad of notes before him, he started dictating and he dictated his speech very rapidly so that it would have rush and spontaneity and the spirit of life. Then he went over this typewritten copy, revised it, inserted, deleted, filled it with pencil marks, and then dictated it all over again. "I never won anything," said he, "without hard labour and the exercise of my best judgment and careful planning and working long in advance."

Often he called in critics to listen to him as he dictated or read his speech to them. He refused to debate with them the wisdom of what he had said. His mind was already made up on that point, and made up irrevocably. He wanted to be told, not what to say, but how to say it. Again and again he went over his typewritten copies, cutting, correcting, improving. That was the speech that the newspapers printed. Of course, he did not memorize it. He spoke extemporaneously. So the talk he actually delivered often differed somewhat from the published and polished one. But the task of dictating and revising was excellent preparation. It made him familiar with his material, with the order of his points. It gave him a smoothness and sureness and polish that he could hardly have obtained in any other fashion.

Sir Oliver Lodge

Sir Oliver Lodge told me that dictating his talks—dictating them rapidly and with substance, dictating them just as if he were actually talking to an audience—he had discovered to be an excellent means of preparation and practise.

Many of the students of this course have found it illuminating to dictate their talks to the dictaphone, and then to listen to themselves. Illuminating? Yes, and sometimes disillusioning and chastening also, I fear. It is a most wholesome exercise. I recommend it.

This practise of actually writing out what you are going to say will force you to think. It will clarify your ideas. It will hook them in your memory. It will reduce your mental wandering to a minimum. It will improve your diction.

Benjamin Franklin

Benjamin Franklin tells in his *Autobiography* how he improved his diction, how he developed readiness in using words and how he taught himself method in arranging his thoughts. This story of his life is a literary classic and, unlike most classics, it is easy to read and thoroughly enjoyable. It is almost a model of plain, straightforward English. Every businessman can peruse it with pleasure and profit. I think you will like the selection I refer to; here it is:

> About this time I met with an odd volume of the *Spectator*. It was the third. I had never before seen any of them. I bought it, read it over and over and was much delighted with it. I thought the writing excellent, and wished, if possible, to imitate it. With this view I took some of the papers, and, making short hints of the sentiment in each sentence laid them by a few days, and then, without looking at the book, try'd to complete the papers again, by expressing each hinted sentiment at length, and as fully as it had been expressed before, in any suitable words that should come to hand. Then I compared my *Spectator* with the original, discovered some of my faults and corrected them. But I found a stock of words, and a readiness in recollecting and using them, which I thought I should have acquired before that time if I had

gone on making verses; since the continual occasion for words of the same import, but of different length, to suit the measure, or of different sounds for the rhyme, would have laid me under a constant necessity of searching for variety, and also have tended to fix that variety in my mind, and make me master of it. Therefore I took some of the tales and turned them back again. I also sometimes jumbled my collections of hints into confusion, and after some weeks endeavoured to reduce them into the best order, before I began to form the full sentences and complete the paper. *This was to teach me method in the arrangement of thoughts.* By comparing my work afterwards with the original, I discovered many faults and amended them; but I sometimes had the pleasure of fancying that, in certain particulars of small import, I had been lucky enough to improve the method of the language, and this encouraged me to think I might possibly in time come to be a tolerable English writer, of which I was extremely ambitious.

PLAY PATIENCE WITH YOUR NOTES

Make notes. Having got your various ideas and illustrations down on scraps of paper, play patience with them—toss them into series of related piles. These main piles ought to represent, approximately, the main points of your talk. Subdivide them into smaller lots. Throw out the chaff until there is nothing but number one wheat left—and even some of the wheat will probably have to be put aside and not used. No man, if he works right, is ever able to use but a percentage of the material he gathers.

One ought never to cease this process of revision until the speech has been made—even then he is very likely to think of points and improvements refinements that ought to have been made.

A good speaker usually finds when he finishes that there have been four versions of his speech: the one that he prepared, the one that he delivered, the one that the newspapers said that he delivered, and the one that he wishes, on his way home, that he had delivered.

TO USE OR NOT TO USE NOTES

Although he was an excellent impromptu speaker, Lincoln, after he reached the White House, never made any address, not even an informal talk to his cabinet, until he had carefully put it all down in writing beforehand. Of course, he was obliged to read his inaugural addresses. The exact phraseology of historical state papers of that character is too important to be left to extemporizing. But, before in Illinois, Lincoln never used to even notes in his speaking. "They always tend to tire and confuse the listener," he said.

And who of us, pray, would contradict him? Don't notes destroy about 50 per cent of your interest in a talk? Don't they prevent, or at least render difficult, a very precious contact and intimacy that ought to exist between the speaker and the audience? Don't they create an air of artificiality? Don't they restrain an audience from feeling that the speaker has the confidence and reserve power that he ought to have?

Make notes, I repeat, during the preparation—elaborate ones, profuse ones. You may wish to refer to them when you are practising your talk alone. You may possibly feel more comfortable if you have them stored away in your pocket when you are facing an audience; but, like the hammer and saw and axe in a train, they should be emergency tools, only for use in the case of a smash-up, a total wreck, threatening death and disaster.

If you must use notes, make them extremely brief and write them in large letters on an ample sheet of paper. Then arrive early at the place where you are to speak and hide your notes behind some books on a table. Glance at them when you must, but endeavour to screen your weakness from the audience. John Bright used to secrete his notes in his big hat lying on the table before him.

However in spite of all that has been said there may be times when it is the part of wisdom to use notes. For example, some men during their first few talks, are so nervous and self-conscious that they are utterly unable to remember their prepared speeches. The result? They shoot off at a tangent, they forget the material they had so carefully rehearsed, they drift off the high road and flounder about in a morass. Why should not such men hold a few very condensed notes in their hands during their maiden efforts?

A child clutches the furniture when it is first attempting to walk, but it does not continue it very long.

DO NOT MEMORIZE WORD FOR WORD

Don't read, and don't attempt to memorize your talk word for word. That consumes time, and courts disaster, Yet, in spite of this warning, some of the men reading these lines will try it; if they do, when they stand up to speak they will be thinking of what? Of their messages? No, they will be attempting to recall their exact phraseology. They will be thinking backwards, not forwards, reversing the usual processes of the human mind. The whole exhibition will be stiff and cold and colourless and inhuman. Do not, I beg of you, waste hours and energy in such futility.

When you have an important business interview, do you sit down and memorize verbatim what you are going to say? Do you? Of course not. You reflect until you get your main ideas clearly in mind. You may make a few notes and consult some records, You say to yourself, "I shall bring out this point and that. I am going to say that a certain thing ought to be done for these reasons...." Then you enumerate the reasons to yourself and illustrate them with concrete cases. Isn't that the way you prepare for a business interview? Why not use the same common sense method in preparing a talk?

REHEARSE

Two thousand years ago, Horace wrote:

> "Seek not for words, seek only fact and thought,
> And crowding in will come the words unsought."

After you have your ideas firmly in mind, then rehearse your talk from beginning to end. Do it silently, mentally, as you walk the street, as you wait for cars and lifts. Get off in a room by yourself and go over it aloud, gesturing, saying it with life and energy. As you practise, imagine there is a real audience before you. Imagine it so strongly that when there is one, it will seem like an old experience. That is the reason why so many criminals are able to go to the scaffold with such bravado; they have already done it so many thousand times in their imagination that they have lost fear of it. When the actual execution does take place, it seems like something that they have gone through very often before.

WHY THE FARMERS THOUGHT LINCOLN "AWFULLY LAZY"

If you practise your talks in this fashion, you will be faithfully following the examples of many famous speakers. Lloyd George, when he was a member of a debating society in his hometown in Wales, often strolled along the country lanes, talking and gesturing to the trees and fence posts.

Lincoln, in his younger days, often walked a round trip of thirty or forty miles to hear a famous speaker like Breckenridge. He came home from these scenes so stirred, so determined to be a speaker that he gathered the other hired workers about him in the fields and, mounting a stump, he made speeches and told them stories. His employers grew angry, declaring that this country Cicero was "awfully lazy", that his jokes and his oratory were ruining the rest of the workers.

Asquith gained his first facility by becoming an active worker in the Union Debating Society in Oxford. Later he organized one of his own. Woodrow Wilson learned to speak in a debating society. So did Henry Ward Beecher. So did the mighty Burke.

Study the careers of famous speakers and you will find one fact that is true of them all: *they practised*. THEY PRACTISED. And the men who make the most rapid progress in this course are those who practise most.

No time for all this? Then do what Joseph Choate used to do. He bought a newspaper of a morning and buried his head in it as he rode to work so no one would bother him. Then, instead of reading the ephemeral scandal and gossip of the day, he thought out and planned his talks.

Chauncey M. Depew led a fairly active life as a railroad president and a United States Senator. Yet, during it all, he made speeches almost every night. "I did not let them interfere with my business," he says. "they were all prepared after I had arrived home from my office late in the afternoon."

We all have three hours a day that we can do with as we please. That was all Darwin had to work with. As he had poor health. Three hours out of twenty-four wisely used, made him famous.

Theodore Roosevelt, when he was in the White House, often had an entire afternoon given over to a series of five-minute interviews, yet he kept a book by his side to utilize even the few spare seconds that came between his engagements.

If you are very busy and pushed for time, read Arnold Bennett's *How To Live On Twenty-Four Hours a Day*. Rip out a hundred pages, put them in your hip pocket, read then during your spare seconds. I got through the book in two days in that fashion. It will show you how to save time, how to get more out of the day.

You must have relaxation and a change from your regular work. That is what the practising of your talks ought to be. If possible, arrange with the other men in this course to meet together an additional night each week for rehearsal. If you cannot do that, play the game of extemporaneous speaking in your own home with your own family.

HOW DOUGLAS FAIRBANKS AND CHARLIE CHAPLIN ENTERTAINED THEMSELVES

It is common knowledge that Douglas Fairbanks and Charlie Chaplin have incomes permitting them to enjoy a little recreation; yet, with all their wealth and fame, they were able to find no greater entertainment, no more enjoyable way of spending their evenings, than by practising extemporaneous speaking.

Here is their story as Douglas Fairbanks told it in the *American Magazine* a few years ago:

> One evening we were fooling and I pretended to introduce Charlie Chaplin at a dinner, he had to rise and make a speech to fit the introduction. And out of that developed a game that we have been playing almost every night for two years. We three (Mary Pickford, Fairbanks, and Chaplin) each write a subject on a slip of paper and fold the slips and shake them up. Each of us draws.

No matter what the word is, each of us has to rise and talk for sixty seconds on that word. We never use the same word again. That's what keeps the stunt new. And we use all kinds of words. I remember one evening when two of the words were 'Faith' and 'Lampshades'. 'Lampshades' fell to me, and I had one of the hardest times I ever had, talking for sixty seconds on "Lampshades'. Just try if you think it is easy. You start out bravely: "Lampshades have two uses. They modify and soften the glare of light, and they are decorative." Then you are through unless you know a lot more about lampshades than I do. I got through somehow. But point is how all three of us have sharpened up since we began that game. We know a lot more about a variety of miscellaneous subjects. But, far better than that, we are learning to assemble our knowledge and thoughts on any topic at a moment's notice and to give it out briefly. We are learning to think on our feet. I say "we are learning", because we are still at this game. We haven't tired of it in almost two years, which means that it is still making us grow.

"Before a speaker faces his audience, he should write a letter to a friend and say: 'I am to make an address on a subject, and I want to make these points.' He should then enumerate the things he is going to speak about in their correct order, if he finds that he has nothing to say in his letter, he had better write to the committee that invited him and say that the probable death of his grandmother will possibly prevent his being present on the occasion."

—Dr. Edward Everett Hale.

"Luck is what happens when preparation meets opportunity."

—Seneca

....

Essential Elements of Successful Speaking

.

*"Life is not easy for any of us. But what of that? We must have
perseverance and above all confidence in ourselves. We must
believe that we are gifted for something, and that this thing,
at whatever cost, must be attained."*

—Marie Curie

Sir Ernest died while steaming southward on the good ship *Quest* to
explore the Antarctic. The first thing that attracted one's eyes on going
aboard the *Quest* were these lines of Kipling engraved on a brass plate:

If you can dream and not make dreams your master;
If you can think and not make thoughts your aim;
If you can meet with triumph and disaster;
And treat those two imposters just the same;
If you can force your heart, and nerve, and sinew
To serve your turn long after they are gone;
And so hold on when there is nothing in you
Except the will which says to them, "Hold on!"
If you can fill the unforgiving minute
With sixty seconds' worth of distance run,
Yours is the earth and everything that's in it,
And, what is more, you'll be a man, my son.

"The spirit of the quest," Shackleton called those verses and, truly, they are the proper spirit with which a man should start out to reach the South Pole or to gain confidence in public speaking.

But that is not the spirit, I regret to add, in which all men begin the study of public speaking. Years ago, when I first engaged in educational work, I was astounded to learn how large a percentage of students who enrolled in night schools of all sorts grew weary and fainted by the wayside before their goals were attained. The number is both lamentable and amazing. It is a sad commentary on human nature.

This is the sixth lesson of this course, and I know from experience that some of the men who are reading these lines are already growing disheartened because they have not, in six short weeks, conquered their fear of audiences, and gained self-confidence. What a pity, for "how poor are they that have not patience. What wound did ever heal but by degrees?"

THE NECESSITY OF PERSISTENCE

When we start to learn any new thing, like French, or golf, or public speaking, we never advance steadily. We do not improve gradually. We do it by sudden jerks, by abrupt starts. Then we remain stationary a time, or we may even slip back and lose some of the ground we have previously gained. These periods of stagnation, or retrogression, are well known by all psychologists; and they have been named "plateaus in the curve of learning". Students of public speaking will sometimes be stalled for weeks on one of these plateaus. Work as hard as they may, they cannot get off it. The weak ones give up in despair. Those with grit persist, and they find that suddenly, overnight, without their knowing how or why it has happened, they have made great progress. They have lifted from the plateau like an aeroplane. Abruptly they have found the knack of the thing. Abruptly they have acquired naturalness and force and confidence in their speaking.

You may always, as we have noted elsewhere in these pages, experience some fleeting fear, some shock, some nervous anxiety the first few moments you face an audience. John Bright felt it to the end of his busy career; so did Gladstone; so did Bishop Wilberforce; so did a score of other eminent speakers. Even the greatest of the musicians have felt it in spite of their innumerable public appearances. Paderewski always fidgeted nervously with his cuffs immediately before he sat down at the piano. Nordica felt her heart racing. So did Sembrich. So did Emma Eames. But it vanished quickly, all of this audience fear, like a mist in the August sunshine.

Their experience will be yours. If you will but persevere, you will soon eradicate everything but this initial fear; and that will be initial fear, and nothing more. After the first few sentences, you will have control of yourself. You will be speaking with positive pleasure.

DON'T GIVE UP

One time a young man who aspired to study law, wrote to Lincoln for advice, and Lincoln replied: "If you are resolutely determined to make a lawyer of yourself, the thing is more than half done already.... Always bear in mind that your own resolution to succeed is more important than any other one thing."

Lincoln knew. He had gone through it all. He had never, in his entire life, had more than a total of one year's schooling. And books? Lincoln once said he had walked and borrowed every book within fifty miles of his home. A long fire was usually kept going all night in the cabin. Sometimes he read by the light of that fire. There were cracks between the logs, and Lincoln often kept a book sticking in a crack. As soon as it was light enough to read in the morning, he rolled over on his bed of leaves, rubbed his eyes, pulled out the book and began devouring it.

He walked twenty and thirty miles to hear a speaker and, returning home, he practised his talks everywhere—in the fields, in the woods, before the crowds gathered at Jones' grocery at Gentryville. He joined literary and debating societies in New Salem and Springfield, and practised speaking on the topics of the day much as you are doing now as a member of this course.

A sense of inferiority always troubled him. In the presence of women he was shy and dumb. When he courted Mary Todd he used to sit in the parlour, bashful and silent, unable to find words, listening while she did the talking. Yet that was the man who, by practise and home study, made himself into the speaker who debated with the accomplished orator, Senator Douglas. That was the man who, at Gettysburg, and again in his second inaugural address, rose to heights of eloquence that have rarely been attained in all the annals of mankind.

Small wonder that, in view of his own terrific handicaps and pitiful struggle, he wrote: "If you are resolutely determined to make a lawyer of yourself, the thing is more than half done already."

There is an excellent picture of Abraham Lincoln in the President's office. "Often when I had some matter to decide," said Theodore Roosevelt, "something involved and difficult to dispose of, something where there were conflicting rights and interests, I would look up at Lincoln, try to imagine him in *my* place, try to figure out what he would do in the same circumstances. It may sound odd to you, but, frankly, it seemed to make my troubles easier of solution."

Why not try Roosevelt's plan? Why not, if you are discouraged and feeling like giving up the fight to make a speaker of yourself, why not pull out of your pocket one of the five dollar notes that bear a likeness of Lincoln, and ask yourself what he would do under the circumstances. You know what he would do. You know what he did do. After he had been beaten by Stephen A. Douglas in the race for the US Senate, he admonished his followers not to "give up after one nor one hundred defeats".

THE CERTAINTY OF REWARD

How I wish I could get you to prop this book open on your breakfast table every morning for a week until you had memorized these words from Professor William James, the famous psychologist:

> Let no youth have any anxiety about the upshot of his education, whatever the line of it may be. If he keeps faithfully busy each hour of the working day, he may safely leave the final result to itself. He can, with perfect certainty, count on waking up some fine morning to find himself one of the competent ones of his generation, in whatever pursuit he may have singled out.

And now, with the renowned Professor James to fall back upon, I shall go so far as to say that if you pursue this course faithfully and with enthusiasm, and keep right on practising intelligently, you may confidently hope to wake up one fine morning and find yourself one of the competent speakers of your city or community.

Regardless of how fantastic that may sound to you now, *it is true a general principle.* Exceptions, of course, there are. A man with an inferior mentality and personality, and with nothing to talk about, is not going to develop into a local Daniel Webster, but, *within reason,* the assertion is correct.

The entire question of your success as a speaker hinges upon only two things—your native ability, and the depth and strength of your desires.

I have known and carefully watched literally thousands of men trying to gain self-confidence and the ability to talk in public. Those that succeeded were, in only a few instances, men of unusual brilliancy. For the most part, they were the ordinary run of businessmen that you will find in your own hometown. But they kept on. Smarter men sometimes got discouraged or too deeply immersed in money making, and they did not get very far, but the ordinary individual with grit and singleness of purpose—at the end of the chapter, he was at the top.

That is only human and natural. Don't you see the same thing occurring all the time in commerce and the professions? Rockefeller said some time ago that the first essential for success in business was patience. It is likewise one of the first essentials for success in this course.

Marshal Foch led to victory by far the greatest army the world has ever seen, and he declared that he had only one virtue; never despairing.

When the French had retreated to the Marne in 1914, General Joffre instructed the generals under him, in charge of two million men, to stop retreating and begin an offensive. This new battle, one of the most decisive in the world's history, had raged for two days when General Foch, in command of Joffre's centre, sent him one of the most impressive messages in military records: "My centre gives way. My right recedes. The situation is excellent. I shall attack."

That attack saved Paris.

So, My dear speaker, when the fight seems hardest and most hopeless, when your centre gives way and your right recedes, "the situation is excellent". Attack! Attack! Attack, and you will save the best part of your manhood—your courage and faith.

CLIMBING THE "WILDER KAISER"

A few summers ago. I started out to scale a peak in the Austrian Alps called the Wilder Kaiser. Baedeker said that the ascent was difficult, and a guide was essential for amateur climbers. We, a friend and I, had none, and we were certainly amateurs, so a third party asked us if we thought we were going to succeed. "Of course," we replied.

"What makes you think so?" he inquired.

"Others had done it without guides," I said, "so I know it is within reason, and *I never undertake anything thinking defeat.*"

As an Alpinist, I am the merest, bungling novice, but that is the proper psychology for anything from essaying public speaking to an assault on Mount Everest.

Think success in this course. See yourself in your imagination talking in public with perfect self-control.

It is easily in your power to do this. Believe that you will succeed. Believe if firmly and you will then do what is necessary to bring success about.

The most valuable thing that most members acquire from a course in public speaking is an increased confidence in themselves, and additional faith in their ability to achieve. And than that, what is more important for one's success in almost any undertaking?

THE WILL TO WIN

Here is a bit of sage advice from Elbert Hubbard that I cannot refrain from quoting. If the average man would only apply and live the wisdom contained in it, he would be happier, more prosperous:

Whenever you go out of doors, draw the chin in, carry the crown of the head high and fill the lungs to the utmost; drink in the sunshine, greet your friends with a smile and put soul into every handclasp. Do not fear being misunderstood and do not waste a minute thinking about your enemies. Try to fix firmly in your mind what you would like to do, and then, without veering off direction, you will move straight to the goal. Keep your mind on the great and splendid things you would like to do, and then, as the days go gliding by, you will find yourself unconsciously seizing upon the opportunities that are required for the fulfillment of your desire, just as the coral insect takes from the running tide the elements it needs. Picture in your mind the table, earnest, useful person you desire to be, and the thought you hold is hourly transforming you into that particular individual.... Thought is supreme. Preserve a right mental attitude—the attitude of courage, frankness and good cheer. To think rightly is to create. All things come through desire and every sincere prayer is answered. We become like that on which our hearts are fixed. Carry your chin in and the crown of your head high. We are gods in the chrysalis.

Napoleon, Wellington, Lee, Grant, Foch—all great military leaders have recognized that an army's will to win and its confidence in its ability to win, do more than any other one thing to determine its success.

"Ninety thousand conquered men," says Marshal Foch, "retire before ninety thousand conquering men only because they have had enough, because they no longer believe in victory, because they are demoralized—at the end of their moral resistance."

In other words, the ninety thousand retiring men are not really whipped physically; but they are conquered because they are whipped mentally, because they have lost their courage and confidence. There is no hope for an army like that. There is no hope for a man like that.

Chaplain Frazier, the ranking chaplain of the US Navy, interviewed those who wished to enlist for the chaplaincy service during the World War. When asked what qualities were essential for the success of a navy chaplain, he replied with four Gs: "Grace, gumption, grit, and *guts*."

Those are also the requisites for success in speaking. Take them as your motto. Take this Robert Service poem as your battle song:

When you're lost in the wild, and you're scared as a child,
And death looks you bang in the eye.
And you're sore as a boil, it's according to Hoyle
To cock your revolver and…die.
But the code of a man, says: "Fight all you can,"
And self-dissolution is barred.
In hunger and woe, oh, it's easy to blow…
It's the hell-served-for-breakfast that's hard.
You're sick of the game! "Well, now, that's a shame."
You're young and you're brave and you're bright.
"You've had a raw deal!" I know—but don't squeal.
Buck up, do your damnedest, and fight.
It's the plugging away that will win you the day.
So don't be a piker, old pard!
Just draw on your grit; it's so easy to quit:
It's the keeping-your-chin-up that's hard.
It's easy to cry that you're beaten—and die.
It's easy to crawfish and crawl;
But to fight and to fight when hope's out of sight,
Why, that's the best game of them all!
And though you come out of each gruelling about
All broken and beaten and scarred,
Just have one more try—it's dead easy to die,
It's the keeping-on-living that's hard.

"I never allow myself to become discouraged under any circumstances…. The three great essentials to achieve anything worthwhile are, first, hard work; second, stick-to-itiveness, third, common sense."

—Thomas A. Edison

"Permanence, perseverance and persistence in spite of all obstacles, discouragement, and impossibilities: It is this, that in all things distinguishes the strong soul from the weak."

—Thomas Carlyle

....

The Improvement of Memory

"Memory...is the diary that we all carry about with us."

—Oscar Wilde

"The average man," says the noted psychologist, Professor Carl Seashore, "Does not use above 10 per cent of his actual inherited capacity for memory. He wastes the 90 per cent by violating the natural laws of remembering."

Are you one of these average men? If so, you are struggling under a handicap both socially and commercially; consequently, you will be interested in, and profit by, reading and rereading this chapter. It describes and explains these natural laws of remembering and shows how to use them in business as well as in speaking.

These "natural laws of remembering" are very simple. There are only three. Every so-called "memory system" has been founded upon them. Briefly, they are *impression repetition,* and *association.*

The first mandate of memory is: get a deep, vivid and lasting *impression* of the thing you wish to retain. And to do that, you must concentrate. Theodore Roosevelt's remarkable memory impressed everyone he met. And no little amount of his extraordinary facility was due to this: his impressions were scratched on steel, not written in water. He had, by persistence and pracrtise, trained himself to concentrate under the most adverse conditions. In 1912, during the Bull Moose Convention in Chicago, his headquarters were in the Congress Hotel. Crowds surged through the street below, crying waving banners, shouting, "We want Teddy!

We want Teddy!" the roar of the throng, the music of bands, the coming and going of politicians, the hurried conferences, the consultations—would have driven the ordinary individual to distraction; but Roosevelt sat in an easy chair in his room, oblivious to it all, reading Herodotus, the Greek historian. On his trip through the Brazilian wilderness, as soon as he reached the camping ground in the evening, he found a dry spot under some huge tree, got out a camp stool and his copy of Gibbon's *Decline and Fall of the Roman Empire*, and, at once, he was so immersed in the book that he was oblivious to the rain, to the noise and activity of the camp, to the sounds of the tropical forest. Small wonder that the man remembered what he read.

Five minutes of vivid, energetic concentration will produce greater results than days of mooning about in a mental haze. "One intense hour," wrote Henry Ward Beecher, "will do more than dreamy years." "If there is any one thing that I have learned which is more important than anything else," says Eugene Grace, president of the Bethlehem Steel Company, "and which I practise every day under any and all circumstances, it is *concentration of the particular job I have in hand.*'

This is one of the secrets of power, especially memory power.

POWER OF OBSERVATION

Thomas Edison found that 27 of his assistants had used, every day for six months, a certain path which led from his lamp factory to the main works at Menlo Park, New Jersey. A cherry tree grew along that path, and yet not one of these 27 men had, when questioned, ever been conscious of that tree's existence.

"The average person's brain," observes Mr. Edison with heat and energy, "does not observe a thousandth part of what the eye observes. It is almost incredible how poor our powers of observation—genuine observation—are."

Introduce the average man to two or three of your friends and, the chances are that two minutes afterwards he cannot recall the name of a single one of them. And why? Because he never paid sufficient attention to them in the first place; he never accurately observed them. He will likely tell you he has a poor memory. No, he has a poor observation.

He would not condemn a camera because it failed to take pictures in a fog, but he expects his mind to retain impressions that are hazy and foggy to a degree. Of course, it can't be done.

The late Mr. Pulitzer, who made the *New York World*, had three words placed over the desk of every man in his editorial offices:

Accuracy

ACCURACY

ACCURACY

That is what we want. Hear the man's name precisely. Insist on it. Ask him to repeat it. Inquire how it is spelled. He will be flattered by your interest and you will be able to remember his name because you have concentrated on it. You have got a clear accurate impression.

THE "BLAB SCHOOL"

Lincoln, in his youth, attended a country school where the floor was made out of split logs: greased pages, torn from the copy books and pasted over the windows. served instead of glass to let in the light. Only one copy of the textbook existed, and the teacher read from it aloud. The pupils repeated the lesson after him, all of them talking at once. It made a constant uproar, and the neighbours called it the "blab school".

At the "blab school", Lincoln formed a habit that clung to him all his life: he forever after read aloud everything he wished to remember. Each morning, as soon as he reached his law office in Springfield, he spread himself out on the couch, hooked one long, ungainly leg over a neighbouring chair, and read the newspaper audibly. "He annoyed me," said his partner, "almost beyond endurance. I once asked him why he read in this fashion. This was his explanation: 'When I read aloud, two senses catch the idea: first, I see what I read; second, I hear it, and therefore I can remember it better'."

His memory was extraordinarily retentive. "My mind," he said, "is like a piece of steel—very hard to scratch anything on it, but almost impossible, after you get it there, to rub it out."

Appealing to two of the senses was the method he used to do the scratching. Go thou, and do likewise....

The ideal thing would be not only to see and hear the thing to be remembered, but to touch it, and smell it, and taste it.

But, above all else, see it. We are visual minded. Eye impressions stick. We can often remember a man's face, even though we cannot recall his name. The nerves that lead from the eye to the brain are twenty times as large as those leading from the ear to the brain. The Chinese have a proverb that says "one time seeing is worth a thousand times hearing".

Write down the name, the telephone number, the speech outline you want to remember. Look at it. Close your eyes. Visualize it in flaming letters of fire.

HOW MARK TWAIN LEARNED TO SPEAK WITHOUT NOTES

The discovery of how to use his visual memory enabled Mark Twain to discard the notes that had hampered his speeches for years. Here is his story as he told it:

Dates are hard to remember because they consist of figures: figures are monotonously unstriking in appearance, and they don't take hold; they form no pictures, and so they give the eye no chance to take hold. Pictures can make dates stick. They can make nearly anything stick—particularly if you make the picture yourself. Indeed, that is the great point—make the picture yourself. I know about this from experience. Thirty years ago I was delivering a memorized lecture every night, and every night I had to help myself with a page of notes to keep from getting myself mixed. The notes consisted of beginnings of sentences, and were eleven in number, and they ran something like this:

In that region the weather—

At that time it was a custom—

But in California one never heard—

Eleven of them. The initialled the brief of the lecture and protected me against skipping. But they all looked about alike on the page; they formed no picture; I had them by heart, but I could never with certainty remember the order of their succession; therefore, I always had to keep those notes by me and look at them every little while. Once I mislaid them; you will not be able to imagine the terrors of that evening. I now saw that I must invent some other protection. So I got ten of the initial letters by heart in their proper order—I, A, B, and so on—and I went on the platform the next night with these marked in ink on my ten finger nails. But it didn't answer. I kept track of the fingers for a while, then I lost it, and after that I was never quite sure which finger I had used last. I couldn't lick off a letter after using it, for while they would have made success certain, it would also have provoked too much curiosity. There was curiosity enough without that. To the audience I seemed more interested in my finger nails than I was in my subject; one or two persons asked afterward what was the matter with my hands.

It was then that the idea of pictures occurred to me! Then my troubles passed away. In two minutes I made six pictures with my pen, and they did the work of the eleven catch-sentences and did it perfectly. I threw the pictures away as soon as they were made, for I was sure I could shut my eyes and see them any time. That was a quarter of a century ago; the lecture vanished out of my head more than twenty years ago, but I could rewrite it form the pictures—for they remain.

I recently had occasion to deliver a talk on memory. I wanted to use, very largely, the material in this chapter. I memorized the points by pictures. I visualized Roosevelt reading history while the crowds were yelling and bands playing outside his window. I saw Thomas Edison looking at a cherry tree. I pictured Lincoln reading a newspaper aloud. I imagined Mark Twain licking ink off his finger nails as he faced an audience.

How did I remember the order of the pictures? By one, two, three, and four? No, that would have been too difficult. I turned these numbers into pictures, and combined the pictures of the numbers with the pictures of the points. To illustrate: number *one* sounds like *run*, so I made a racehorse stand for *one*. I pictured Roosevelt in his room, reading astride a racehorse. For *two*, I chose a word that sounds like two—*zoo*. I had the cherry-tree that Thomas Edison was looking at standing in the bear cage at the zoo. For *three,* I pictured an object that sounds like *three*—tree. I had Lincoln sprawled out in the top of a tree, reading aloud to his partner. For *four* I imagined a picture that sounds like four—*door.* Mark Twain stood at an open door, leaning against the jamb, licking the ink off his fingers as he talked to the audience.

I realize full well that many men who read this will think that such a method verges on the ridiculous. It does. That is one reason why it works. It is comparatively easy to remember the bizarre and ridiculous. Had I tried to remember the order of my points by numbers only, I might easily have forgotten; but by the system I have just described, it was almost impossible to forget. When I wished to recall my third point, I had but to ask myself what was in the top of the tree. Instantly I saw Lincoln.

I have, very largely for my own convenience, turned the numbers from one to twenty into pictures, choosing pictures that sound like the numbers. I have set them down here. If you will spend half an hour memorizing these picture-numerals you will then be able, after having a list of twenty objects called to you but once, to repeat them in their exact order and to skip about at random announcing which object was called to you eighth, which fourteenth, which third, and so on.

Here are the picture numbers. Try the test. You will find it decidedly amusing.

1. Run—visualize a race horse.
2. Zoo—see the bear cage in the zoo.
3. Tree—picture the third object called to you as lying in the top of a tree.
4. Door—or wild boar. Take any object or animal that sounds like four.
5. Beehive.
6. Sick—see a Red Cross nurse.
7. Heaven—a street paved with gold, and angles playing on harps.
8. Gate.

9. Wine—the bottle has fallen over on the table, and the wine is streaming out and pouring down on something below. Put action into the pictures. It helps to make them stick.

10. Den of wild animals in a rocky cave in the deep woods.

11. A football eleven, rushing madly across the field. I picture them carrying aloft the object that I wish to recall as number eleven.

12. Shelve—see someone shoving something back on a shelf.

13. Hurting—see the blood spurting out of a wound and reddening the thirteenth object.

14. Courting—a couple are sitting on something and making love.

15. Lifting—a strong man, a regular John L. Sullivan, is lifting something high above his head.

16. Licking—a fist night.

17. Leaving—a housewife is kneading dough, and into the dough she needs the seventeenth object.

18. Waiting—a woman is standing at a forked path in the deep woods for someone.

19. Pining—a woman is weeping. See her tears falling on the nineteenth thing you wish to recall.

20. Horn of plenty—a goat's horn overflowing with flowers and fruit and corn.

If you wish to try the test, spend a few minutes memorizing these picture-numbers. If you prefer, make pictures of your own. For ten, think of *wren* or fountain *pen* or *hen* or *sen-sen*—anything that sounds like ten. Suppose that the tenth object recalled to you a windmill. See the hen sitting on the windmill, or see it pumping ink to fill the fountain pen. Then, when you are asked what was the tenth object called, do not think of ten at all; but merely ask yourself where was the hen sitting. You may not think it will work, but try it. You can soon astound people with what they will consider to be an extraordinary capacity for remembering. You will find it entertaining if nothing else.

MEMORIZING A BOOK AS LONG AS
THEY NEW TESTAMENT

One of the largest universities in the world is the El Hazar at Cairo. It is a Mohammedan institution with twenty-one thousand students. The entrance examination requires every applicant to repeat the Koran from memory. The Koran is about as long as the New Testament, and three days are required to recite it!

The Chinese students, or "study boys" as they are called, have to memorize some of the religious and classical books of China.

How are these Arab and Chinese students—many of them men of mediocre ability—able to perform these apparently prodigious feats of memory?

By *repetition,* the second "natural law of remembering".

You can memorize an almost endless amount of material if you will repeat it often enough. Go over the knowledge you want to remember. Use it. Apply it. Employ the new word in your conversation. Call the stranger by his name if you want to remember it. Talk over in conversation the points you want to make in your public address. The knowledge that is used tends to stick.

THE KIND OF REPETITION THAT COUNTS

But the mere blind, mechanical going over a thing by rote is not enough. Intelligent repetition, repetition done in accordance with certain well-established traits of the mind—that is what we must have. For example, Professor Ebbinghaus gave his students a long list of nonsense syllables to memorize, such as "deyux", "qoli", and so on. He found that these students memorized as many of these syllables by thirty-eight repetitions, distributed over a period of three days, as they did by sixty-eight repetitions done at a single sitting. Other psychological tests have repeatedly shown similar results.

This is a very significant discovery about the working of our memories. It means that we know now that the man who sits down and repeats a thing over and over until he finally fastens it in his memory, is using twice as much time and energy as is necessary to achieve the same results when the repeating process is done at judicious intervals.

This peculiarity of the mind—if we can call it such—can be explained by two factors:

First, during the intervals between repetitions, our subconscious minds are busy making the associations more secure. As Professor William James sagely remarks: "We learn to swim during the winter and to skate during the summer."

Second, the mind, coming to the task at intervals, is not fatigued by the strain of an unbroken application. Sir Richard Burton, the translator of the *Arabian Nights*, spoke twenty-seven languages like a native: yet he confessed that he never studied or practised any language for more than fifteen minutes at a time, "for, after that, the brain lost its freshness."

Surely, now, in the face of these facts, no man who prides himself on his common sense, will delay the preparation of a talk until the night before it is to be given. If he does, his memory will, of necessity, be working at only one-half its possible efficiency.

Here is a very helpful discovery about the way in which we forget. Psychological experiments have repeatedly shown that of the new material we have learned, we forget more during the first eight hours than during the next thirty days. An amazing ratio! So, immediately before you go into a business conference, immediately before you make a speech, look over your data, think over your facts, refresh your memory.

Lincoln knew the value of such a practise, and employed it. The scholarly Edward Everett preceded him on the programme of speech-making at Gettysburg. When he saw that Everett was approaching the close of his long, formal oration, Lincoln "grew visibly nervous, as he always did when another man was speaking and he was to follow". Hastily adjusting his spectacles, he took his manuscript from his pocket and read it silently to himself to refresh his memory.

PROFESSOR WILLIAM JAMES EXPLAINS
THE SECRET OF A GOOD MEMORY

So much for the first two laws of remembering. The third one, *association,* however, is the indispensable element in recalling. In fact, it is the explanation of memory itself. "Our mind is," as Professor James has sagely observed,

> essentially an associating machine... Suppose I am silent for a moment, and they say in commanding accents: 'Remember! Recollect!' Does your faculty of memory obey the order, and reproduce any definite image from your past? Certainly not. It stands staring into vacancy, and asking, 'What kind of thing do you wish me to remember?' It needs, in short, a cue. But, if I say, remember the date of your birth, or remember what you had for breakfast, or remember the succession of notes in the musical scale; then your faculty of memory immediately produces the required result: the *cue* determines its vast set of potentialities toward a particular point. And if you now look to see how this happens, you immediately perceive that the *cue* is something contiguously associated with the thing recalled. The words, 'date of my birth,' have an ingrained association with a particular number, month, and year; the words, 'breakfast this morning,' cut off all other lines or recall except those which lead to coffee and bacon and eggs; the words, 'musical scale,' are inveterate mental neighbours of do, re, mi, fa, sol, la, etc. The laws of association govern, in fact, all the trains of our thinking which are not interrupted by sensations breaking on us from without. Whatever appears in the mind must be *introduced;* and, when introduced, it is as the associate of something already there. This is as true of what you are recollecting as it is of everything else you think of.... An educated memory depends upon an organized system of associations, and its goodness depends on two of their peculiarities: first, on the persistency of the associations; and, second, on their number.... The 'secret of a good memory' is thus the secret of forming diverse and multiple associations with every fact we care to retain. But

this forming of associations with a fact—what is it but thinking about the fact as much as possible? Briefly, then, of two men with the same outward experiences, *the one who thinks over his experiences most,* and weaves them into the most systematic relations with each other, will be the one with the best memory.

HOW TO LINK YOUR FACTS TOGETHER

Very good, but how are we to set about weaving our facts into systematic relations with each other? The answer is: by finding their meaning, by thinking them over. For example, if you will ask and answer these questions about any new fact, that process will help to weave it into a systematic relation with other facts.

a) Why is this so?

b) How is this so?

c) When is it so?

d) Where is it so?

e) Who said it is so?

If it is a stranger's name, for example, and it is a common one, we can perhaps tie it to some business friend who bears the same name. On the other hand, if it is unusual, we can take occasion to say so. This often leads the stranger to talk about his name. For example: while writing this chapter, I was introduced to a Mrs. Soter. I requested her to spell the name and remarked upon its unusualness. "Yes," she replied, "it is very uncommon. It is a Greek word meaning 'the Saviour'." Then she told me about her husband's people who had come from Athens and of the high positions they had held in the government there. I have found it quite easy to get people to talk about their names, and it always helps me to remember them.

Observe the stranger's looks sharply. Note the colour of his eyes and his hair, and look closely at his features. Note how he is dressed. Listen to his manner of talking. Get a clear, keen, vivid impression of his looks and personality, and associate these with his name. The next time these sharp impressions return to your mind, they will help bring the name with them.

Haven't you had the experience, when meeting a man for the second or third time, to discover that although you could remember his business or profession, you could not recall his name? The reason is this: a man's business is something definite and concrete. It has a meaning. It will adhere like a court plaster while his meaningless name will roll away like hail falling on a steep roof. Consequently, to make sure of your ability to recall a man's name, fashion a phrase about it that will tie up to his business. There can be no doubt whatever about the efficacy of this method. For example, twenty men, strangers to one another, recently met in an Athletic Club to study this course. Each man was asked to rise, announce his name and business. A phrase was then manufactured to connect the two; and, within a few minutes, each person present could repeat the name of every other individual in the room. Even to the end of the course, neither the names nor businesses were forgotten, for they were linked together. They adhered.

Here are the first ten names, in alphabetical order, from that group, and here are the crude phrases that were used to tie the names to the businesses:

Mr. G.P. Albrecht (sand business)—"Sand makes all bright."

Mr. George A. Ansley (real estate)—"To sell real estate, advertise an *Ansley's Magazine."*

Mr. G.W. Bayliss (asphalt)—"Use asphalt and pay less."

Mr. H.M. Biddle (woollen cloth)—"Mr. Biddle piddles about the wool business."

Mr. Gideon Boericke (mining)—"Boericke bores quickly for mines."

Mr. Thomas J. Devery (printing)—"Every man needs Devery's printing."

Mr. O.W. Doolittle (automobiles)—"Do little and you won't succeed in selling cars."

Mr. Thomas Fischer (coal)—"He fishes for coal orders."

Mr. Frank H. Goldey (lumber)—"There is gold in the lumber business."

Mr. J.H. Hancock (*Saturday Evening Post*)—"Sign your John Hancock to a subscription blank for the *Saturday Evening Post.*"

HOW TO REMEMBER DATES

Dates can best be retained by connecting them with important dates already firmly established in the mind. Isn't it far more difficult, for example, for an American to remember that the Suez Canal was opened in 1869 than to remember that the first ship passed through it four years after the close of the Civil War? If an American tried to remember that the first settlement in Australia was made in 1788, the date is likely to drop out of his mind like a loose bolt out of a car; it is far more likely to stick if he thinks of it in connection with July 4, 1776, and remembers that it occurred twelve years after the Declaration of Independence. That is like screwing a nut on the loose bolt. It holds.

It is well to bear this principle in mind when you are selecting a telephone number. For example, the writer's phone number, during the last was, was 1776. No one had difficulty in remembering it. If you can secure from the phone company some such number as 1942, 1861, 1865, 1914, 1918, your friends will not have to consult the directory. They might forget that your phone number was 1942, if you gave them the information in a colourless fashion; but would it slip their minds if you said, "You can easily remember my phone number; 1492, the year Columbus discovered America."

The Australians, New Zealanders, and Canadians who are reading these lines would, of course, substitute for 1776, 1861, 1865 significant dates in their own history.

What is the best way to memorize the following dates?

a) 1564—Birth of Shakespeare.

b) 1607—The first English settlement in America was made in James-town.

c) 1819—The birth of Queen Victoria.

d) 1807—The birth of Robert E. Lee.

e) 1789—The Bastile was destroyed.

You would doubtlessly find it tiresome to memorize, by sheer mechanical repetition, the names of the thirteen original states in the order in which they entered the Union. But tie them together with a story and the memorizing can be done with a fraction of the time and trying. Read the following paragraph just once. Concentrate, When you have finished, see if you cannot name the thirteen states in their correct order:

> One Saturday afternoon, a young lady from Delaware bought a ticket over the Pennsylvania railroad for a little outing. She packed a New Jersey sweater in her suitcase, and visited a friend, Georgia, in Connecticut. The next morning the hostess and her visitor attended Mass in a church on Mary's land. Then they took the south car-line home, and dined on a new ham, which had been roasted by Virginia, the coloured cook, from New York. After Dinner they took the North car line and rode to the island.

HOW TO REMEMBER THE POINTS OF YOUR TALK

There are only two ways by which we can possibly think of a thing: first, by means of an *outside stimulus;* second, by *association* with something already in the mind. Applied to speeches, that means just this: first, you can recall your points by the aid of some outside stimulus such as notes—but who likes to see a speaker use notes? Second, you can remember your points by associating them with something already in the mind. They should be arranged in such a logical order that the first one leads inevitably to the second, and the second to the third as naturally as the door of one room leads into another.

That sounds simple, but it may not prove so for the beginner whose thinking powers are rendered *hors de combat* with fear. There is, however, a method of tying our points together that is easy, rapid, and all but foolproof. I refer to the use of a nonsense sentence. To illustrate: suppose you wish to discuss a veritable jumble of ideas, unassociated and hence hard to remember, such as, for example, *cow, cigar, Napoleon, house, religion.* Let us see if we cannot weld those ideas like the links of a chain by means of this absurd sentence: "The cow smoked a cigar and hooked Napoleon, and the house burned down with religion."

Now, will you please cover the above sentence with your hand while you answer these questions? What is the third point in that talk, the fifth, fourth, second, first?

Does the method work? It does! And the members of this course are urged to use it.

Any group of ideas can be linked together in some such fashion, and the more ridiculous the sentence used for the linking, the easier it will be to recall.

WHAT TO DO IN CASE OF A COMPLETE BREAKDOWN

Let us suppose that, in spite of all his preparation and precaution, a speaker, in the middle of his talk, suddenly finds his mind a blank—suddenly finds himself staring at his hearers completely balked, unable to go on—a terrifying situation. His pride rebels at sitting down in confusion and defeat— He feels that he might be able to think of his next point, of some point, if he had only ten, fifteen seconds of grace; but even fifteen seconds of frantic silence before an audience would be little less than disastrous. What is to be done? When a certain well-known US Senator recently found himself in this situation he asked his audience if he were speaking loudly enough; if he could be heard distinctly in the back of the room. He knew that he was. He was not seeking information. He was seeking time. And in that momentary pause, he grasped his thought and proceeded.

But perhaps the best life-saver in such a mental hurricane is this: use the last word, or phrase, or idea in your last sentence for the beginning of a new sentence. This will make an endless chain that, like Tennyson's brook and, I regret to say, with as little purpose as Tennyson's brook, will run on for ever. Let us see how it works in practise. Let us imagine that a speaker, talking on Business Success, finds himself in a blind mental alley after having said: "The average employee does not get ahead because he takes so little real interest in his work, displays so little initiative."

"*Initiative*". Start a sentence with "*initiative*". You will probably have no idea of what you are going to say or how you are going to end the sentence, but, nevertheless, begin. Even a poor showing is more to be desired than utter defeat.

"Initiative means originality, doing a thing on your own, without eternally waiting to be told."

That is not a scintillating observation. It won't make speech history. But isn't it better than an agonizing silence? Our last phrase was what?—"waiting to be told." All right, let us start a new sentence with that idea.

"The constant telling and guiding and driving of employees who refuse to do any original thinking is one of the most exasperating things imaginable."

Well, we got through that one. Let us plunge again. This time we must say something about imagination:

"Imagination—that is what is needed. Vision. "Where there is no vision,' Solomon said, 'the people perish'."

We did two that time without a hitch. Let us take heart and continue:

"The number of employees who perish each year in the battle of business is really lamentable. I say lamentable, because with just a little more loyalty, a little more ambition, a little more enthusiasm, these same men and women might have lifted themselves over the line of demarcation between success and failure. Yet the failure in business never admits that this is the case."

And so on…. While the speaker is saying these platitudes off the top his mind, he should, at the same time, be thinking hard of the next point in his planned speech, of the thing he had originally intended to say.

This endless chain method of talking will, if continued very long, trap the speaker into discussing plum pudding or the price of canary birds. However, it is a splendid first aid to the injured mind broken down temporarily through forgetfulness: and, as such, it has been the means of resuscitating many a gasping and dying speech.

WE CANNOT IMPROVE OUR MEMORIES FOR ALL CLASSES OF THINGS

I have pointed out in this chapter how we may improve our *methods* of getting vivid impressions, of repeating and of tying our facts together. But memory is so essentially a matter of association that "there can be", as Professor James points out, "no improvement of the general or elementary faculty of memory; there can only be improvement of our memory for special systems of associated things."

By memorizing, for instance, a quotation a day from Shakespeare, we may improve our memory for literary quotations to a surprising degree. Each additional quotation will find many friends in the mind to tie to. But the memorizing of everything from Hamlet to Romeo will not necessarily aid one retaining facts about the cotton market or the Bessemer process for desiliconizing pig iron.

Let us repeat: if we apply and use the principles discussed in this chapter, we will improve our *manner* and efficiency for memorizing anything, but, if we do not apply these principles, then the memorizing of ten million facts about football will not help us in the slightest in memorizing facts about the stock market. Such unrelated data cannot be tied together. "Our mind is essentially an associating machine."

"Memory is the greatest of artists, and effaces from your mind what is unnecessary."

—Maurice Baring

"It is safe to say that the businessman's most immediate need is a serviceable memory."

—E.B. Gowin

CHAPTER 8

···

The Secret of Good Delivery

"Instructions for making a speech: be sincere, be brief, be seated."

—Franklin D. Roosevelt

Shortly after the close of the last war, I met two brothers in London, Sir Ross and Sir Keith Smith. They had just made the first aeroplane flight from London to Australia, had won the fifty thousand dollar prize offered by the Australian government, had created a sensation throughout the British Empire, and had been knighted by the King.

Captain Hurley, a well-known scenic photographer, had flown with them over a part of their trip, taking motion pictures; so I helped them prepare in illustrated travel talk of their flight and trained them in the delivery of it. They gave it twice daily for four months in Philharmonic Hall, London, one speaking in the afternoon and the other at night.

They had had identically the same experience, had sat side by side as they flew halfway around the world, and they delivered the same talk almost word for word. Yet, somehow it didn't sound like the same talk at all.

There is something besides the mere words in a talk which counts. It is the flavour with which they are delivered. "It is not so much what you say as how you say it."

I once sat beside a young woman at a public concert who was reading, as Paderewski played them, the notes of a Mazurka by Chopin. She was mystified. She couldn't understand. His fingers were touching precisely the same notes that hers had touched when she had played it; yet her rendition had been commonplace, and his was inspired, a thing of surpassing beauty, a performance that held the audience enthralled. It was not the mere notes that be touched, it was the way he touched them, a feeling, an artistry, a personality that he put into the touching that made all the difference between mediocrity and genius.

The same thing holds true when one is touching words. There is an old saying in the English Parliament that everything depends upon the manner in which one speaks and not upon the matter, Quintilian said that long ago when England was one of the outlying colonies of Rome.

Like most old sayings, it needs to be taken *cum grano salis*, but good delivery will make very thin matter go a very long away. I have often noticed in college contests that it is not always the speaker with the best material who wins. Rather, it is the speaker who can talk so well that his material sounds best.

"Three things matter in a speech," Lord Morley once observed with gay cynicism, "who says it, how he says it, and what he says—and, of the three, the last matters the least." An exaggeration? Yes, but scratch the surface of it and you will find the truth shining through.

Edmund Burke wrote speeches so excellent in logic and reasoning and composition that they are today studied as classic models of oration in half the colleges of the land; yet Burke, as a speaker, was a notorious failure. He didn't have the ability to deliver his gems, to make them interesting and forceful; so he was called "the dinner bell" of the House of Commons. When he arose to talk, the other members coughed and shuffled and went out in droves.

You can throw a steel-jacketed bullet at a man with all your might, and you cannot make even a dent in his clothing. But put powder behind a tallow candle and you can shoot it through a pine board. Many a tallow-candle speech with powder makes, I regret to say, more of an impression than a steel-jacketed talk with no force behind it.

Look well, therefore, to your delivery.

THE ART OF DELIVERY

What does a department store do when it "delivers" the article you have bought? Does the driver just toss the package into the backyard and let it go at that? Is merely getting a thing out of one's own hands the same as getting it delivered? The messenger boy with a telegram delivers the "wire" into the direct possession of the person for whom it is intended. But do all speakers?

Let me give you an illustration that is typical of the fashion in which thousands of men talk. I happened on one occasion to be stopping in Mürren, a summer resort in the Swiss Alps. I was living at a hotel operated by a London company, and they usually sent out from England a couple of lecturers each week to talk to the guests. One of them was a well-known English novelist. Her topic was "The Future of the Novel". She admitted that she had not selected the subject herself; and the long and short of it was that she had nothing to say about it that she really cared enough about saying to make it worth while expressing. She had hurriedly made some rambling notes, and she stood before the audience ignoring her hearers, not even looking at them, staring sometimes over their heads, sometimes at her notes, sometimes at the floor. She called off her words into the primeval void with a faraway look in her eyes and a faraway ring in her voice.

That kind of performance isn't delivering a talk at all. It is a soliloquy. It has no sense of communication. And that is the first essential of good talking: *a sense of communication.* The audience must feel that there is a message being delivered straight from the mind and heart of the speaker to their minds and their hearts. The kind of talk I have just described might just as well have been spoken out in the sandy, waterless wastes of the Gobi desert. In fact, it sounded as if it were being delivered in some such spot rather than to a group of living human beings.

This matter of delivering a talk is, at the same time, a very simple and a very intricate process. It is also a very much misunderstood and abused one.

THE SECRET OF GOOD DELIVERY

An enormous amount of nonsense and twaddle has been written about delivery. Is has been shrouded in rules and rites and made mysterious. Old-fashioned "elocution", that abomination in the sight of God and man, has often made it ridiculous.

The businessman, going to the library or bookshop, has found volumes on "oratory" that were utterly useless. In spite of progress in other directions, in almost every state in the Union today, schoolboys are still being forced to recite the ornate "oratory" of Webster and Ingersoll—a thing that is as much out of style as far removed from the spirit of this age as the hats worn by Mrs. Ingersoll and Mrs. Webster would be if they were resurrected today.

An entirely new school of speaking has sprung up since the Civil War. In keeping with the spirit of the times, it is as modern as the *Saturday Evening Post*, direct as a telegram, businesslike as an automobile advertisement. The verbal fireworks that were once the vague would no longer be tolerated by an audience in this year of grace.

A modern audience, regardless of whether it is fifteen people at a business conference or a thousand people under a tent, wants the speaker to talk just as directly as he would in a chat, and in the same general manner that he would employ in speaking to one of them in conversation.

In the same *manner*, but not with the same amount of force. If he tries that, he will hardly be heard. In order to appear natural he has to use much more energy in talking to forty people than he does in talking to one; just as a statue on top of a building has to be of heroic size in order to make it appear of lifelike proportions to an observer on the ground.

At the close of Mark Twain's lecture in a Nevada mining camp, an old prospector approached him and inquired: "Be them your natural tones of eloquence?"

That is what the audience wants: "your natural tones of eloquence," enlarged a bit.

Speak to the Chamber of Commerce just as you would to John Henry Smith. What is a meeting of the Chamber of Commerce, after all, but a mere collection of John Henry Smiths? Won't the same methods that are successful with those men individually be successful with them collectively?

I have just described the delivery of a certain novelist. In the same ballroom in which she had spoken, I had the pleasure, a few nights later, of hearing Sir Oliver Lodge. His subject was "Atoms and Worlds". He had devoted to it more than half a century of thought and study and experiment and investigation. He had something that was essentially a part of his heart and mind and life, something that he wanted very much to say. He forgot—and I, for one, thanked God that he did forget—that he was trying to make a speech. That was the least of his worries. He was concerned only with telling the audience about atoms, telling us accurately and lucidly and feelingly. He was earnestly trying to get us to see what he saw and to feel what he felt.

And what was the result? He delivered a remarkable talk. It had both charm and power. It made a deep impression. He was a speaker of unusual ability. Yet I am sure he didn't regard himself in that light. I am sure that few people who heard him ever think of him as a public speaker at all.

If you, my dear reader, speak in public so that people hearing you will suspect that you have had training in public speaking, you will not be a credit to your instructor. He desires you to speak with such intensified and exalted naturalness that your auditors will never dream that you have been trained. A good window does not call attention to itself. It merely lets in the light. A good speaker is like that. He is so natural that his hearers never notice his manner of speaking; they are conscious only of his matter.

STEPHEN A. DOUGLAS V. ABRAHAM LINCOLN

"All Fords are exactly alike," their maker used to say, but no two men are just alike. Every new life is a new thing under the sun; there has never been anything just like it before, and never will be again. A young man ought to get that idea about himself; he should look for the single spark of individuality that makes him different from other folks, and develop that for all he is worth. Society and schools may try to iron it out of him; their tendency is to put us all in the same mould, but I say don't let that spark be lost; it's your only real claim to importance.

All that is doubly true of public speaking. There is no other human being in the world like you. Hundreds of millions of people have two eyes and a nose and a mouth, but none of them look precisely like you; and none of them have exactly your traits and methods and cast of mind. Few of them will talk and express themselves just as you do when you are speaking naturally. In other words, you have an individuality. As a speaker, it is your most precious possession. Cling to it. Cherish it. Develop it. It is the spark that will put force and sincerity into your speaking. "It is your only real claim to importance."

Sir Oliver Lodge spoke differently from other men, because he himself was different. The man's manner of speaking is as essentially a part of his own individuality as are his beard and bald head. If he had tried to imitate Lloyd George, he would have been false, he would have failed.

The most famous debates ever held in America took place in 1858 in the prairie towns of Illinois between Senator Stephen A. Douglas and Abraham Lincoln. Lincoln was tall and awkward. Douglas was short and graceful. These men were as unlike in their characters and mentality and personalities and dispositions as they were in their physiques.

Douglas was the cultured man of the world. Lincoln was the rail splitter who went to the front door on his sock feet to receive company. Douglas' gestures were graceful. Lincoln's were ungainly. Douglas was utterly destitute of humour. Lincoln was one of the greatest storytellers who ever lived. Douglas seldom used a simile. Lincoln constantly argued by analogy and illustration. Douglas was haughty and overbearing. Lincoln was humble and forgiving. Douglas thought in quick flashes. Lincoln's mental processes were much slower. Douglas spoke with the impetuous rush of a whirlwind. Lincoln was quieter and deeper and more deliberate.

Both of these men, unlike as they were, were able speakers because they had the courage and good sense to be themselves. If either had tried to imitate the other, he would have failed miserably. But each one, by using to the utmost his own peculiar talents, made himself individual and powerful. *Go thou and do likewise.*

That is an easy direction to give. But is it an easy one to follow? Most emphatically it is not. As Marshal Foch said of the art of war: "It is simple enough in its conception, but unfortunately complicated in its execution."

It takes practise to be natural before an audience. Actors know that. When you were a little boy, four years old, you probably could, had you but tried, have mounted a platform and "recited" naturally to an audience. But when you are twenty-and-four, or forty-and-four, what will happen if you mount a platform and start to speak? Will you retain that unconscious naturalness that you possessed at four? You may, but it is dollars to dough-nuts that you will become stiff and stilted and mechanical, and draw back into your shell like a snapping turtle.

The problem of teaching or of training men in delivery is not one of superimposing additional characteristics; it is largely one of removing impediments, of freeing men, of getting them to speak with the same naturalness that they would display if someone were to knock them down.

Hundreds of times I have stopped speakers in the midst of their talks and implored them to "talk like a human being". Hundreds of nights I have come home mentally fatigued and nervously exhausted from trying to drill and force men to talk naturally. No, believe me, it is not so easy as it sounds.

And the only way under high Heaven by which you can get the knack of this enlarged naturalness is by practise. And, as you practise, if you find yourself talking in a stilted manner, pause and say sharply to yourself mentally: "Here! What is wrong? Wake up. Be human." Then pick out some man in the audience, some man in the back, the dullest looking chap you can find, and talk to him. Forget there is anyone else present at all. *Converse* with him. Imagine that he has asked you a question and that you are answering it. If he were to stand up and talk to you, and you were to talk back to him, that process would immediately and inevitably make your talking more conversational, more natural, more direct. So, imagine that that is precisely what is taking place.

You may go so far as to actually ask questions and answer them. For example, in the midst of your talk, you may say, "and you ask what proof have I for this assertion? I have adequate proof and here it is..." Then proceed to answer the imaginary question. That sort of thing can be done very naturally; it will make it direct and pleasant and conversational.

Sincerity and enthusiasm and high earnestness will help you too. When a man is under the influence of his feelings, his real self comes to the surface. The bars are down. The heat of his emotions has burned all barriers away. He acts spontaneously. He talks spontaneously. He is natural.

So, in the end, even this matter of delivery comes back to the thing which has already been emphasized repeatedly in these pages: namely, put your heart in your talks.

"I shall never forget," said Dean Brown in his lectures on Preaching before the Yale Divinity School.

The description given by a friend of mine of a service which he once attended in the city of London. The preacher was George McDonald. He read for the Scripture lesson that morning the eleventh chapter of Hebrews. When the time came for the sermon, he said: "You have all heard about these men of faith. I shall not try to tell you what faith is. There are theological professors who could do that much better than I could do it. I am here to help you believe." Then followed such a simple, heartfelt and majestic manifestation of the man's own faith in those unseen realities which are eternal, as to beget faith in the minds and hearts of all hearers. *His heart was in his work. And his delivery was effective because it rested back upon the genuine beauty of his own inner life.*

"His heart was in his work." That is the secret. Yet I know that advice like this not popular. It seems vague. It sounds indefinite. The average student wants foolproof rules. Something definite. Something he can put his hands on. Rules are precise as the directions for operating a car.

That is what he wants. That is what I would like to give him. It would be easy for him. It would be easy for me. There are such rules, and there is only one little thing wrong with them: they don't work. They take all the naturalness and spontaneity and life and juice out of a man's speaking. I know. In my younger days I wasted a great deal of energy trying them. They won't appear in these pages for, as Josh Billings observed in one of his lighter moments: "There ain't no use in knowin' so many things ain't so."

FEATURES OF NATURAL SPEAKING

We are going to discuss here some of the features of natural speaking in order to make them more clear, more vivid. I have hesitated about doing it, for someone is almost sure to say: "Ah, I see, just force myself to do these things and I'll be all right." No, you won't. *Force* yourself to do them and you will be all wooden and all mechanical.

You used most of these principles yesterday in your conversation, used them as unconsciously as you digested your dinner last night. That is the way to use them. It is the *only* way. And it will come, as far as public speaking is concerned, as we have already said, only by practice.

FIRST

STRESS IMPORTANT WORDS, SUBORDINATE UNIMPORTANT ONES

In conversation, we hit one syllable in a word, and hit it hard, and hurry over the others like a pay car passing a string of hoboes. For example, MassaCHUsetts afFLICtion, atTRACtiveness, enVIRonment. We do almost the same thing with a sentence. We make one or two important words tower up like a skyscraper.

This is not a strange or unusual process I am describing. Listen. You can hear it going on about you all the time. You yourself did it a hundred. Maybe a thousand, times yesterday. You will doubtless do it a hundred times tomorrow.

Here is an example. Read the following quotation, striking the works in big type hard. Run over the others quickly. What is the effect?

"I have SUCCEEDED in whatever I have undertaken, because I have WILLED it. I have NEVER HESITATED which has given me an ADVANTAGE over the rest of mankind."—Napoleon.

This is not the only way to read these lines. Another speaker would do it differently perhaps. There are no ironclad rules for emphasis. It all depends.

Read these selections aloud in an earnest manner, trying to make the ideas clear and convincing. Don't you find yourself stressing the big, important words and hurrying over the others?

> *If you think you are beaten, you are.*
> *If you think you dare not, you don't.*
> *If you'd like to win, but think you can't,*
> *It's almost a cinch you won't.*
> *Life's battles don't always go*
> *To the stronger or faster man;*
> *But soon or late the man who wins*
> *Is the one who thinks he can.*

—Anonymous

SECOND

CHANGE YOUR PITCH

The pitch of our voices in conversation flows up and down the scale from high to low and back again, never resting, but always shifting like the face of the sea. Why? No one knows, and no one cares. The effect is pleasing, and it is the way of nature. We never had to learn to do this: it come to us as children, unsought and unaware, but let us stand up and face audience, and the chances are our voices will become as dull and flat and monotonous as the alkali deserts.

When you find yourself talking in a monotonous pitch—and usually it will be a high one—just pause for a second and say to yourself: "I am speaking like a wooden Indian. *Talk* to these people. Be human. Be natural."

Will that kind of lecture to yourself help you any? A little, perhaps. The pause itself will help you. You have to work out your own salvation by practice.

You can make any phrase or word that you choose stand out like a green bay-tree by either suddenly lowering or raising your pitch on it. Dr. Cadman, the famous Congregational minister, often did it. So does

Sir Oliver Lodge. So did Bryan. So did Roosevelt, So does almost every speaker of note.

In the following quotations, try saying the italicized words in a much lower pitch than you use for the rest of the sentence. What is the effect?

> *"I have but one merit, that of never despairing."*
>
> —Marshal Foch

> *"I have lived eighty-six years. I have watched men climb up to success, hundreds of them, and of all the elements that are important for success, the most important is faith."*
>
> —Cardinal Gibbons

THIRD

Vary Your Rate of Speaking

When a little child talks, or when we talk in ordinary conversation, we *constantly change our rate of speaking.* It is pleasing. It is natural. It is unconscious. It is emphatic. It is, in fact, one of the very best of all possible ways to make an idea stand out prominently.

Walter B. Stevens, in his *Reporter's Lincoln,* issued by the Missouri Historical Society, tell us that this was one of Lincoln's favourite methods of driving a point home:

> He would speak several words, with great rapidity, come to the word or phrase he wished to emphasize, and let his voice linger and bear hard on that, and then he would rush to the end of his sentence like lightning.... He would devote as much time to the word or two he wished to emphasize as he did to half a dozen less important words following it.

Such a method invariably arrests attention. To illustrate: I have often quoted in a public talk the following statement by Cardinal Gibbons. I wanted to emphasize the idea of courage; so I lingered on these italicized words, drew them out and spoke as if I myself were impressed with them—and I was. Will you please read the selection aloud, trying the same method and note the results.

A short time before his death, Cardinal Gibbons said: I have lived *eighty-six years*. I have watched men *climb* up to *success, hundreds* of them, and of all the elements that are *important* for success, the *most important* is *faith. No great thing comes to any man unless he has courage."

Try this: say "thirty million dollars" quickly and with an air of triviality so that is sounds like a very small sum. Now, say "thirty thousand dollars": say it slowly, say it feelingly, say it as if you were tremendously impressed with the hugeness of the amount. Haven't you now made the thirty thousand sound larger than the thirty million?

FOURTH
Pause Before and After Important Ideas

Lincoln often paused in his speaking. When he had come to a big idea that he wished to impress deeply on the minds of his hearers, he bent forward, looked directly into their eyes for a moment and said nothing at all. This sudden silence had the same effect as a sudden noise: It attracted notice. It made everyone attentive, alert, awake to what was coming next. For example, when his famous debates with Douglas were drawing to a close, when all the indications pointed to his defeat, he became depressed, his old habitual melancholy stealing over him at times, and imparting to his words a touching pathos. In one of his concluding speeches, he suddenly *"stopped and stood silent for a moment*, looking round upon the throng of half-indifferent, half-friendly faces before him, with those deep-sunken weary eyes that always seemed full of unshed tears. Folding his hands, as if they too were tired of the helpless flight, he said, in his peculiar monotone: 'My friends, it makes little difference, very little difference, whether Judge Douglas or myself elected to the United States Senate, but the great issue which we have submitted to you today is far above and beyond any personal interests or the political fortunes of any man. And my friends,' here he paused again, and the audience were intent on every word, 'that issue will live and breathe and burn when the poor, feeble, stammering tongues of Judge Douglas and myself are silent in the grave'."

"These simple words," relates one of his biographers, "and the manner in which they were spoken, touched every heart to the core."

Lincoln also paused after the phrase he wanted to emphasize. He added to their force by keeping silent while the meaning sank in and effected its mission.

Sir Oliver Lodge paused frequently in his speaking, both before and after important ideas; paused as often as three or four times in one sentence, but he did it naturally and unconsciously. No man, unless he were analyzing Sir Oliver's methods, would have noticed it.

"By your silence," says Kipling. "ye shall speak." Nowhere is silence more golden than when it is judiciously used in talking.

It is a powerful tool, too important to be ignored, yet it is usually neglected by the beginning speaker.

In the following excerpt from Holman's *Ginger Talks,* I have marked the places where a speaker might profitably pause. I do not say that these are the *only* places where one ought to pause, or even the best places. I say only that it is *one* way of doing it. Where to pause is not a matter of hard and fast rules. It is a matter of meaning and temperament and feeling. You might pause one place in a speech today, and in another place in the same speech tomorrow.

Read this selection aloud without pausing; then read it again, making the pauses I have indicated. What is the effect of the pause?

"Selling goods is a battle," (pause and let the idea of *battle* soak in) "and only fighters can win in it." (Pause and let that point soak in.) "We may not like these conditions, but we didn't have the making of them and we can't alter them." (Pause.) "Take your courage with you when you enter the selling game." (Pause.) "If you don't," (pause and lengthen out suspense for a second) "you'll strike out every time you come to bat, and score nothing higher than a string of goose eggs." (Pause). "The fellow who knocks the cover of the ball or lifts it over the fence is always the chap who steps up to the plate" (pause and increase the suspense as to what you are going to say about this extraordinary player) "with grim determination in his heart."

A speaker may follow the directions I have set down in this lesson and still have a hundred faults. He may talk in public just as he does in conversation and consequently, he may speak with an unpleasant voice and make grammatical errors and be awkward and offensive and do a score of unpleasant things. A man's natural method of every day talking may need a vast number of improvements. Perfect your natural method of talking in conversation, and then carry that method to the platform.

> *"The mastery of forceful speech is one of the noblest purposes to which a man can address himself."*
>
> **—Newell Dwight Hillis**

> *"Perhaps there is no more important component of character than steadfast resolution. The boy who is going to make a great man, or is going to count in any way in after-life, must make up his mind not merely to overcome a thousand obstacles, but to win in spite of a thousand repulses and defeats."*
>
> **—Theodore Roosevelt**

CHAPTER 9

....

Platform Presence and Personality

*"Let the counsel of thine own heart stand, for no man is more
faithful unto thee then it. It is sometimes wont to show thee
more than seven watchmen who sit above in a high tower."*

—Rudyard Kipling

The Carnegie Institute of Technology at one time gave intelligence tests
to one hundred prominent businessmen. The tests were similar to those
used in the army during the war, and the results led the institute to declare
that personality contributes more to business success than does superior
intelligence.

That is a very significant pronouncement: very significant for the
businessman, very significant for the educator, very significant for the
professional man, very significant for the speaker.

Personality—with the exception of preparation—is probably the
most important factor in public address. "In eloquent speaking," declared
Elbert Hubbard, "it is manner that wins, not words." Rather it is manner
plus ideas. But personality is a vague and elusive thing, defying analysis
like the perfume of the violet. It is the whole combination of the man, the
physical, the spiritual, the mental; his traits, predilections, his tendencies,
his temperament, his cast of mind, his vigour, his experience, his training,
his life. It is as complex as Einstein's theory of relativity, almost as little
understood.

A man's personality is very largely the result of his inheritances. It is
largely determined before birth. True, his later environment has something

to do with it. But, all in all, it is an extremely difficult factor to alter or improve. Yet we can, by taking thought, strengthen it to some extent and make it more forceful, more attractive. At any rate, we can strive to get the utmost possible out of this strange thing that nature has given us. The subject is of vast importance to every one of us. The possibilities for improvement, limited as they are, are still large enough to warrant a discussion and investigation.

If you wish to make the most of your individuality, go before your audience rested. A tired man is not magnetic nor attractive. Don't make the all-too-common error of putting off your preparation and your planning until the very last moment, and then working at a furious pace, trying to make us for lost time. If you do, you are bound to store up bodily poisons and brain fatigues that will prove terrific drags, holding you down, snapping your vitality, weakening both your brain and your nerves.

If you must make an important talk to a committee meeting at four, do not, if you can well avoid it, come back to the office after lunch. Go home, if possible, have a light lunch and the refreshment of a siesta. Rest— that is what you need—physical and mental and nervous.

When you have to make an important talk, beware of young hunger. Eat as sparingly as a saint. On Sunday afternoons, Henry Ward Beecher used to have biscuits and milk at five, and nothing after that.

"When I am singing in the evening," said Madame Melba, "I do not dine but have a very light repast at five o'clock, consisting of either fish, chicken, or sweetbread, with a baked apple and a glass of water. I always find myself hungry for supper when I get home from the opera or concert."

How wisely Melba and Beecher acted, I never realized until after I became a professional speaker myself and tried to deliver a two-hour talk each evening having consumed a hearty meal.

Experience taught me that I couldn't enjoy a *filet de sole aux pommes nature* and follow that by a beef-steak and fried potatoes and salad and vegetables and a sweet, and then stand up an hour afterwards and do either myself or my subject or my body justice. The blood that ought to have been in my brain was down in my stomach wrestling with that steak and potatoes. Paderewski was right: he said when he ate what he wanted to eat before a concert, the animal in him got uppermost, that it even got into his fingertips and clogged and dulled his playing.

WHAT MAKES A GOOD SPEAKER

Do nothing to dull your energy. It is magnetic. Vitality, aliveness, enthusiasm: they are among the first qualities I have always sought for in employing speakers and instructors of speaking. People cluster around the energetic speaker, the human dynamo of energy, like wild geese around a field of autumn wheat.

I have often seen this illustrated by the open air speakers in Hyde Park, London. A spot near Marble Arch entrance is a rendezvous for speakers of every creed and colour. On a Sunday afternoon, one can take his choice and listen to a Catholic explaining the doctrine of the infallibility of the Pope, to a Socialist propounding the economic gospel of Karl Marx, to an Indian explaining why it is right and proper for a Mohammedan to have four wives, and so on. Hundreds crowd about one speaker, while his neighbour has only a handful. Why? Is the topic always an adequate explanation of the disparity between the drawing powers of different speakers? No. More often the explanation is to be found in the speaker himself: he is more interested and, consequently interesting. He talks with more life and spirit. He radiates vitality and animation; they always challenge attention.

THE IMPORTANCE OF GROOMING

An inquiry was sent to a large group of people by a psychologist and university president, asking them the impression clothes made on them. All but unanimously, they testified that when they were well groomed and faultlessly and immaculately attired, the knowledge of it, the feeling of it, had an effect which, while it was difficult to explain, was still very definite, very real. It gave them more confidence, brought them increased faith in themselves, and heightened their self-respect. They declared that when they had the look of success they found it easier to think success, to achieve success. Such is the effect of clothes on the wearer himself.

What effect do they have on an audience? I have noticed time and again that if a speaker has baggy trousers, shapeless coat and footwear, fountain pen and pencils peeping out of his breast pocket, a newspaper or a pipe and tin of tobacco bulging out the sides of his garment—I have noticed that an audience has as little respect for that man as he has for his own appearance. Aren't they very likely to assume that his mind is as sloppy as his unkempt hair and unpolished shoes?

BEING IN THE SPOTLIGHT

When General Lee came to Appomattox Court House to surrender his army, he was immaculately attired in a new uniform and, as his side, hung a sword of extraordinary value. Grant was coatless, swordless, and was wearing the shirt and trousers of a private. "I must have contrasted very strangely," he wrote in his *Memoirs,* "with a man so handsomely dressed, six feet high, and of faultless form." The fact that he had not been appropriately attired for this historic occasion came to be one of the real regrets of Grant's life.

The Department of Agriculture has several hundred stands of bees on its experimental farm. Each hive has a large magnifying glass built into it, and the interior can be flooded with electric light by pressing a button; so, any moment, night or day, these bees are liable to be subject to the minutest scrutiny. A speaker is like that: he is under the magnifying glass, he is in the spotlight, all eyes are upon him. The smallest disharmony in his personal appearance now looms up like a mountain from the plains.

"HE WHO CANNOT SMILE OUGHT NOT TO KEEP A SHOP"

A number of years ago, I was writing the life story of a certain banker for a magazine. I asked one of his friends to explain the reason for his success. No small amount of it, he said, was due to the man's winning smile. At first thought, that may sound like exaggeration but I believe it is really true. Other men, scores of them, hundreds of them, may have had more experience and as good financial judgment, but he had an additional asset they didn't possess—he had a most agreeable personality. And a warm, welcoming smile was one of the striking features of it. It gained one's confidence immediately. It secured one's goodwill instantly. We all want to see a man like that succeed, and it is a real pleasure to give him our patronage.

"He who cannot smile," says a Chinese proverb, "ought not to keep a shop." And isn't a smile just as welcome before an audience as behind a counter? I am thinking now of a particular student who attended a course in public speaking conducted by a Chamber of Commerce. He always came out before the audience with an air that said he liked to be there, that he loved the job that was before him. He always smiled and acted as if he were glad to see us, and so immediately and inevitably his hearers warmed towards him and welcomed him.

But I have seen speakers—students of this course, I regret to admit—who walked out before the other members in a cold, perfunctory manner as if they had a disagreeable task to perform, and that, when it was over, they would thank God. We in the audience were soon feeling the same way. These attitudes are contagious.

SEAT YOUR AUDIENCE TOGETHER

As a public lecturer, I have frequently spoken to a small audience scattered through a large hall in the afternoon, and to a large audience packed into the same hall at night. The evening audience has laughed heartily at the same things that brought only a smile to the faces of the afternoon group; the evening crowd has applauded generously at the very places where the afternoon gathering was utterly unresponsive. Why?

For one thing, the elderly women and the children that are likely to come in the afternoon cannot be expected to be as demonstrative as the more vigorous and discriminating evening crowd; but that is only a partial explanation.

The fact is that no audience will be easily moved when it is scattered. Nothing so dampens enthusiasm as wide open spaces and empty chairs between the listeners.

Henry Ward Beecher said in his *Lectures on Preaching:*

People often say, "Do you not think it is much more inspiring to speak to a large audience than a small one? No, I say. I can speak just as well to twelve persons as to a thousand, provided those twelve are crowded around me and close together, so that they can touch each other. But even a thousand people with four feet of space between every two of them, would be just the same as an empty room.... Crowd your audience together and you will set them off with half the effort.

A man in a large audience tends to lose his individuality. He becomes a member of the crowd and is swayed far more easily than he would be as a single individual. He will laugh at and applaud things that would leave him unmoved if he were only one of half a dozen people listening to you.

It is far easier to get people to act as a body than to act singly. Men going into battle, for example, invariably want to do the most dangerous and reckless thing in the world—they want to huddle together. During the late war, German soldiers were known to go into battle at times with their arms locked about one another.

Crowds! Crowds! Crowds! They are a curious phenomenon. All great popular movements and reforms have been carried forward by the aid of the crowd mentality. An interesting book on this subject is Everett Dean Martin's *The Behaviour of Crowds.*

If we are going to talk to a small group, we should choose a small room. Better to pack the aisles of a small place than to have people scattered through the lonely, deadening spaces of a large hall.

If your hearers are scattered, ask them to move down front and be seated near you. Insist on this, before you start speaking.

Unless the audience is a fairly large one, and there is a real reason, a necessity, for the speaker standing on a platform, don't do so. Get down on the same level with them. Stand near them. Break up all formality. Get an intimate contact. Make the thing conversational.

OPEN THE WINDOWS

Keep the air fresh. In the well-known process of public speaking, oxygen is just as essential as the larynx, pharynx and human epiglottis. All the eloquence of Cicero, and all the feminine pulchritude in Ziegfeld's Follies, could hardly keep an audience awake in a room poisoned with bad air. So, when I am one of a number of speakers, before beginning. I almost always ask the audience to stand up and rest for two minutes while the windows are thrown open.

For fourteen years Major James B. Pond travelled all over the United States and Canada as manager for Henry Ward Beecher when that famous preacher was at his flood tide as a popular lecturer. Before the audience assembled, Pond always visited the hall or church or theatre where Beecher was to appear, and rigorously inspected the lighting, seating, temperature and ventilation. Pond had been a blustering, roaring old army officer and he loved to exercise authority; so if the place was too warm or the air was dead and he could not get the windows open, he hurled books through them, smashing and shattering the glass. He believed with Spurgeon that "the next best thing to the Grace of God for a preacher is oxygen".

LET LIGHT SHINE ON YOUR FACE

Unless you are demonstrating spiritualism before a group of people, flood the room, if possible, with lights, it is as easy to domesticate a quail as to develop enthusiasm in a half-lighted room gloomy as the inside of a thermos bottle.

Read David Belasco's articles on stage production, and you will discover that the average speaker does not have the foggiest shadow of the ghost of an idea of the tremendous importance of proper lighting.

Let the light strike your face. People want to see you. The subtle changes that ought to play across your features are a part, and a very real part, of the process of self-expression. Sometimes they mean more than your words. If you stand directly under a light, your face may be dimmed by a shadow; if you stand directly in front of a light, it is sure to be. Would it not, then, be the part of wisdom to select, before you arise to speak, the spot that will give you the most advantageous illumination?

NO TRUMPERY ON THE PLATFORM

And do not hide behind a table. People want to look at the whole man. They will even lean out in the aisles to see all of him.

Some well-meaning soul is pretty sure to give you a table and a water pitcher and a glass; but if your throat becomes dry, a pinch of salt or a taste of lemon will start the saliva again better than Niagara.

You do not want the water nor the pitcher. Neither do you want all the other useless and ugly impedimenta that clutter up the average platform.

The sales rooms of the various automobile makers are beautiful, orderly, pleasing to the eye. The Paris offices of the large perfumers and jewellers are artistically and luxuriously appointed. Why? It is good business. One has more respect, more confidence, more admiration for a concern housed like that.

For the same reason, a speaker ought to have a pleasing background. The Ideal arrangement to my way of thinking, would be no furniture at all. Nothing behind the speaker to attract attention or at either side of him—nothing but a curtain of dark blue velvet.

But what does he usually have behind him? Maps and signs and tables, perhaps a lot of dusty chairs, some piled on top of the others. And what is the result? A cheap, Slovenly, disorderly atmosphere, So clear all the trumpery away.

"The most important thing in public speaking," said Henry Ward Beecher, "is the man."

So let the man stand out like the snow clad top of the Jungfrau towering against the blue skies of Switzerland.

NO GUESTS ON THE PLATFORM

I was once in London, Ontario, when the Prime Minister of Canada was speaking. Presently the janitor, armed with a long pole, started to ventilate the room, moving about from window to window. What happened?

The audience, almost to a man, ignored the speaker for a little while and stared at the janitor as intently as if he had been performing some miracle.

An audience cannot resist—or, what comes to the same thing, it *will not* resist—the temptation to look at moving objects. If a speaker will only remember that truth, he can save himself some trouble and needless annoyance.

First, he can refrain from twiddling his thumbs, playing with his clothes and making little nervous movements that detract from him. I remember seeing a New York audience watch a well-known speaker's hands for half an hour while he spoke and played with the covering of a pulpit at the same time.

Second, the speaker should arrange, if possible, to have the audience seated so they won't have their attention distracted by seeing the latecomers enter.

Third, he should have no guests on the platform. A few years ago Raymond Robins delivered a series of talks. I, along with a number of others, was invited to sit on the platform with him. I declined on the ground that it was unfair to the speaker. I noted the first night how many of these guests shifted about and put one leg over the other and back again, and so on; and every time one of them moved, the audience looked away from the speaker to the guest. I called Mr. Robins' attention to this the next day; and during the reminder of his evenings with us, he very wisely occupied the platform alone.

David Belasco did not permit the use of red flowers on the stage because they attract too much attention. Then why should a speaker permit a restless human being to sit facing the audience while he talks? He shouldn't. And, if he is wise, he won't.

THE ART OF SITTING DOWN

Isn't it well for the speaker himself not to sit facing the audience before he begins? Isn't it better to arrive as a fresh exhibit than an old one?

But, if we *must* sit, let us be careful of *how* we sit. You have seen men look round to find a chair with the modified movements of a foxhound lying down for the night. They turned round and when they did locate a chair, they doubled up and flopped down into it with all the self-control of a sack of sand.

A man who knows how to sit feels the chair strike the back of his legs, and, with his body easily erect from head to hips, he *sinks* into it with his body under perfect control.

POISE

We just said, a few pages previously, not to play with your clothes because it attracted attention. There is another reason also. It gives an impression of weakness, a lack of self-control. Every movement that does not add to your presence detracts from it. There are no neutral movements. None. So stand still and control yourself physically and that will give you an impression of mental control, of poise.

After you have risen to address your audience, do not be in a hurry to begin. That is the hallmark of the amateur. Take a deep breath. Look over your audience for a moment; and, if there is a noise or disturbance, pause until it quiets down.

Hold your chest high. But why wait until you get before an audience to do this? Why not do it daily in private? Then you will do it unconsciously in public.

"Not one man in ten," says Luther H. Gulick in his book *The Efficient Light,* "carries himself so as to look his best.... Keep the neck pressed against the collar." Here is a daily exercise he recommends: "Inhale slowly and as strongly as possible. At the same time press the neck back firmly against the collar. Now hold it there hard. There is no harm in doing this in an exaggerated way. The object is to "straighten out that part of the back which is directly between the shoulders. This deepens the chest."

And what shall you do with your hands? Forget them. If they fall naturally to your sides, that is ideal. If they feel like a bunch of bananas to you, do not be deluded into imagining that anyone else is paying the slightest attention to them or has the slightest interest in them.

They will look best hanging relaxed at your sides. They will attract the minimum of attention there. Not even the hypercritical can criticize that position. Besides, they will be unhampered and free to flow naturally into gestures when the urge makes itself felt.

But suppose that you are very nervous and that you find putting them behind your back or shoving them into your pockets helps to relieve your self-consciousness—what should you do? Use your common sense. I have heard a number of celebrated speakers of this generation. Many, if not most, put their hands into their pockets occasionally while speaking. Bryan did it. Chauncey M. Depew did it. Teddy Roosevelt did it. Even so fastidious a dandy as Disraeli sometimes succumbed to this temptation. But the sky did not fall and, according to the weather reports, if my memory serves me right, the sun came up on time as usual the next morning. If a man has something to say worthwhile, and says it with contagious conviction, surely it will matter little what he does with his hands and feet, if his head is full and heart stirred, these secondary details will very largely take care of themselves. After all, the stupendously important thing in making a talk is the psychological aspect of it, not the position of the hands and feet.

ABSURD ANTICS TAUGHT IN THE NAME OF GESTURE

And this brings us very naturally to the much-abused question of gesture. My first lesson in public speaking was given by the president of a college in the middle west. This lesson, as I remember it, was chiefly concerned with gesturing; it was not only useless but misleading and positively harmful. I was taught to let my arm hang loosely at my side palm facing the rear, fingers half closed and thumb touching my leg. I was drilled to bring the arm up in a graceful curve, to make a classical swing with the wrist and then to unfold the forefinger first, the second finger next, and the little finger last. When the whole aesthetic and ornamental movement had been executed, the arm was then to retrace the same graceful and unnatural curve and rest again by the side of the leg. The whole performance was wooden and affected. There was nothing sensible or honest about it. I was drilled to act as no man in his right mind ever acted anywhere.

There was no attempt whatever to get me to put my own individuality into my movements; no attempt to spur me on to feeling like gesturing; no endeavour to get the flow and blood of life in the process, and make it natural and unconscious and inevitable; no urging me to let go, to be spontaneous, to break through my shell of reserve, to talk and act like a human being. No, the whole regrettable performance was as mechanical as a typewriter, as lifeless as a last year's bird nest, as ridiculous as a Punch and Judy show.

That was in 1902. It seems incredible that such absurd antics could have been taught in the twentieth century, but they are still going on. Only a few years ago a whole book about gesturing was published by a professor teaching in one of the large colleges of the East—a whole book trying to make automatons out of men, telling them which gesture to make on this sentence, which to make on that, which to make with one hand, which with both, which to make high, which to make medium, which to make low, how to hold this finger and how to hold that. I have seen twenty men at a time standing before a class, all reading the same ornate oratorical selections from such a book, all making precisely the same gestures on precisely the same words, and all making themselves precisely ridiculous. Artificial, time-killing, mechanical, injurious—it has brought this whole subject into disrepute with many men. The dean of a large college in Massachusetts recently said that his institution had no course in public speaking because he had never seen one that was practical, one that taught men to speak sensibly. My sympathy was all with the dean.

Nine-tenths of the stuff that has been written on gestures has been a waste and worse than a waste of good white paper and good black ink. Any gesture out of a book is very likely to look like it. The place to get it is out of yourself, out of your heart out of your mind, out of your own interest in the subject, out of your own desire to make someone else see as you see, out of your own impulses. The only gestures that are worth one, two, three, are those that are born on the spur of the instant. An ounce of spontaneity is worth a ton of rules.

Gesture is not a thing to be put on at will like a dinner jacket. It is merely an outward expression of inward condition just as are kisses and colic and laughter and sea sickness.

And a man's gestures, like his toothbrush, should be very personal things. And, as all men are different, their gestures will be individual if they will only act naturally.

No two men should be drilled to gesture in precisely the same fashion. In the last chapter, I discussed the difference between Lincoln and Douglas as speakers. Imagine trying to make the long, awkward, slow-thinking Lincoln gesture in the same fashion as did the rapidly-talking, impetuous and polished Douglas. It would be ridiculous.

"Lincoln," according to his biographer and law partner, Herndon, "did not gesticulate as much with his hands as with his head. He used the latter frequently, throwing it with vim this way and that. This movement was a significant one when he sought to enforce his statement. It sometimes came with a quick jerk, as if throwing off electric sparks into combustible material. He never sawed the air or rent space into tatters and rags as some orators do. He never acted for stage effect.... As he moved along in his speech, he became freer and less uneasy in his movements; to that extent he was graceful. He had a perfect naturalness, a strong individuality, and to that extent he was dignified, he despised glitter, show, set forms, and shams.... There was a world of meaning and emphasis in the long, bony finger of his right hand as he dotted the ideas on the minds of his hearers. Sometimes, to express joy or pleasure, he would raise both hands at an angle of about fifty degrees, the palms upward, as if desirous of embracing the spirit of that which he loved. If the sentiment was one of detestation—denunciation of slavery, for example—both arms, thrown upward and fists clenched, swept through the air, and he expressed an execration that was truly sublime. This was one of his most effective gestures, and signified most vividly a fixed determination to drag down the object of his hatred and trample it in the dust. He always stood squarely on his feet, toe even with toe; that is, he never put one foot before the other. He neither touched nor leaned on anything for support. He made but few changes in his positions and attitudes. He never ranted, never walked backward and forward on the platform. To else his arms, he frequently caught hold, with his left hand of the lapel of his coat, keeping his thumb upright and leaving his right hand free to gesticulate." St. Gaudens caught him in just that attitude in the statue facing Westminster Abbey.

Such was Lincoln's method. Theodore Roosevelt was more vigorous, fiery, active, his whole face alive with feeling, his fist clenched, his entire body an instrument of expression. Bryan often used the outstretched hand with open palm. Gladstone often struck a table or his open palm with his fist, or stamped his foot with a resounding thud on the floor. Lord Rosebery used to raise his right arm and bring it down with a bold sweep that had tremendous force. Ah, but there was force first in the speaker's thoughts and convictions; that was what made the gesture strong and spontaneous.

Spontaneity... life... they are the *summum bonum* of action. Burke was angular and exceedingly awkward in his gestures. Pitt sawed the air with his arms "like a clumsy clown". Sir Henry Irving handicapped by a lame leg and decidedly old movements. Lord Macauley's actions on the platform were ungainly. So were Grattan's. So were Parnell's. "The answer then appears to be," said the late Lord Curzon at Cambridge University, in an address on Parliamentry Eloquence, "that great public speakers make their own gestures; and that while a great orator is doubtless aided by a handsome exterior and graceful action, it does not matter very much if he happens to be ugly and awkward."

Some years ago, I heard the famous Gypsy Smith preach. I was enthralled by the eloquence of this man who has led so many thousands to Christ. He used gestures—lots of them—and was no more conscious of them than of the air he breathed. Such is the ideal way.

And such is the way you, my dear reader, will find yourself making gestures if you will but practise and apply the principles already enunciated in this course. I can't give you any rules for gesturing, for everything depends upon the temperament of the speaker, upon his preparation, his enthusiasm, his personality, the subject the audience, the occasion.

SOME SUGGESTIONS

Here are, however, a few limited suggestions that may prove useful. Do not repeat one gesture until it becomes monotonous. Do not make short, jerky movements from the elbow. The movements from the shoulder look better on the platform. Do not end your gestures too quickly. If you are using the index finger to drive home you thought, do not be afraid to hold that gesture through an entire sentence. The failure to do this is a very common error and a serious one. It distorts your emphasis, making small things unimportant, and truly important points seem trivial by comparison.

When you are doing real speaking before a real audience, make only the gestures that come natural. But while you are practising before the members of this course, *force* yourself, if necessary, to use gestures. Force yourself to do it and the doing of it will so awaken and stimulate you that your gestures will soon be coming unsought.

Shut your book. You can't learn gestures from a printed page. Your own impulses, as you are speaking, are more to be trusted, more valuable than anything any instructor can possibly tell you.

If you forget all else we have said about gesture and delivery, remember this: if a man is so wrapped up in what he has to say, if he is so eager to get his message across that he forgets himself and talks and acts spontaneously, then his gestures and his delivery, unstudied though they may be, are very likely up to a man and knock him down. You will probably discover that, when he regains his feet, the talk he delivers will be well nigh flawless as a gem of eloquence.

Here are the best eleven words I have ever read on the subject of delivery:

Fill up the barrel.

Knock out the bung.

Let nature caper.

*"Action is eloquence, and the eyes of the ignorant
are more learned than their ears."*

—Shakespeare

*"There is often as much eloquence in the tone of the voice, in
the eyes, and in the air of a speaker as in his choice of words."*

—La Rochefoucauld

....

How to Make Your Meaning Clear

"Be brief, be pointed, let your matter stand lucid in order, solid and at hand; spend not your words on trifles but condense; strike with the mass of thought, not drops of sense; press to the close with vigor, once begun, and leave – how hard the task."

—Joseph Story

A famous English bishop, during the last war, spoke to some unlettered negro troops. They were on their way to the trenches; but a very small percentage of them had any adequate idea why they were being sent. I know: I questioned them. Yet the Lord Bishop to talked these negroes about "international amity" and "Servia's right to a place in the sun". Why, the half of those negroes did not know whether Servia was a town or a disease. He might as well, as far as results were concerned, have delivered a sonorous eulogy on the Nebular Hypothesis. However, not a single trooper left the hall while he was speaking: the military police with revolvers were stationed at every exit to prevent that consummation.

I do not wish to belittle the bishop. He is every inch a scholar, and before a body of collegiate men he would probably have been powerful, but he failed with these negroes, and he failed utterly: he did not know his audience, and he evidently knew neither the precise purpose of his talk not how to accomplish it.

What do we mean by the purpose of an address? Just this: every talk, regardless of whether the speaker realizes it or not, has one of four major goals. What are they?

1. To make something clear.
2. To impress and convince.
3. To get action.
4. To entertain.

Let us illustrate these by a series of concrete examples.

Lincoln, who was always more or less interested in mechanics, one invented and patented a device for lifting stranded boats off sand bars and other obstructions. He worked in a mechanic's shop near his law office, making a model of his apparatus. Although the device finally came to naught, he was decidedly enthusiastic over its possibilities. When friends came to his office to view the model, he took no end of pains to explain it. The main purpose of those explanations was clearness.

When he delivered his immortal oration at Gettysburg, when he gave his first and second inaugural addresses, when Henry Clay died and Lincoln delivered an eulogy of his life—on all these occasions, Lincoln's main purpose was impressiveness and conviction. He had to be clear, of course, because he could be convincing; but, in these instances, clearness was not his major consideration.

In his talks to juries, he tried to win favourable decisions. In his political talks, he tried to win votes. His purpose, then, was *action*.

Two years before he was elected President, Lincoln prepared a lecture on Inventions. His purpose was entertainment. At least, that should have been his goal, but he was evidently not very successful in attaining it. His career as a popular lecturer was, in fact, a distinct disappointment. In one town, not a person came to hear him.

But he did succeed and he succeeded famously in the other speeches of his that I have referred to. And why? Because, in those instances, he knew his goal, and he knew how to achieve it. He knew where he wanted to go and how to get there. And because so many speakers don't know just that, they often flounder and come to grief.

For example: I once saw a United States Congressman hooted and hissed and forced to leave the stage of the old New York Hippodrome, because he had—unconsciously, no doubt, but nevertheless, unwisely—chosen clearness as his goal. It was during the last war. He talked to his audience about how the United States was preparing. The crowd did not want to be instructed. They wanted to be entertained. They listened to him patiently, politely, for ten minutes, a quarter of an hour, hoping the performance would come to a rapid end. But it didn't. He rambled on and on; patience snapped and the audience would not stand for more. Someone began to cheer ironically. Others took it up. In a moment, a thousand people were whistling and shouting. The speaker, obtuse and incapable as he was of sensing the temper of his audience, had the bad taste to continue. That aroused them. A battle was on. Their impatience mounted to ire. They determined to silence him. Louder and louder grew their storm of protest. Finally, the roar of it, the anger of it drowned his words—he could not have been heard twenty feet away. So he was forced to give up, acknowledge defeat, and retire in humiliation.

Profit by his example. Know your goal. Choose it wisely before you set out to prepare your talk. Know how to reach it. Then set about it, doing it skilfully and with science.

All this requires knowledge, special and technical instruction. The remainder of this chapter will show you how to make your talks clear.

USE COMPARISONS TO PROMOTE CLEARNESS

As to clearness: do not underestimate the importance of it nor the difficulty. I recently heard a certain Irish poet give an evening of readings from his own poems. Not 10 per cent of the audience, half the time, knew what he was talking about. Many talkers, both in public and private are a lot like that.

When I discussed the essentials of public speaking with Sir Oliver Lodge, a man who has been lecturing to university classes and to the public for forty years, he emphasized most of all the importance, first, of knowledge and preparation, and second, of "taking good pains to be clear".

The great General Von Moltke, at the outbreak of the Franco-Prussian War, said to his officers: "Remember, gentlemen, that any order that *can* be misunderstood, *will* be misunderstood."

Napoleon recognized the same danger. His most emphatic and oft-re-iterated instruction to his secretaries was: "Be clear! Be clear!"

When the disciples asked Christ why He taught the public by parables, He answered: "Because they seeing, see note: and hearing, hear not; neither do they understand."

And when you talk on a subject strange to your hearer or hearers, can you hope that they will understand you any more readily than people understood the Master?

Hardly. So what can we do about it? What did He do when confronted by a similar situation? Solved it in the most simple and natural manner imaginable: described the things people did not know by likening them to things they did know. The kingdom of Heaven...what would it be like? How could those untutored peasants of Palestine know? So Christ described it in terms of subjects and actions with which they were already familiar:

> The kingdom of Heaven is like unto leaven, which a woman took, and hid in three measures of meal, till the whole was leavened.
>
> Again, the kingdom of heaven is like unto a merchantman seeking goodly pearls...
>
> Again, the kingdom of heaven is like unto a net that was cast into the sea....

That was lucid; they could understand that. The housewives in the audience were using leaven every week; the fishermen were casting their nets into the sea daily; the merchants were dealing in pearls.

And how did David make clear the watchfulness and loving kindness of Jehovah?

"The lord is my shepherd, I shall not want. He maketh me to lie down in green pastures, He leadeth me beside the still waters...."

Green grazing grounds in that almost barren country... still waters where the sheep could drink—those pastoral people could understand that.

Here is a rather striking and half-amusing example of the use of this principle: some missionaries were translating the Bible into the dialect of a tribe near equatorial Africa. They progressed to the verse: "Though your sins be as scarlet, they shall be white as snow." How were they to translate that? Literally? Meaningless. Absurd. The natives had never scooped snow off the pathway on a February morning. They did not even have a word for snow. They could not have told the difference between snow and coal tar, but they had climbed coconut trees many times and shaken down a few nuts for lunch; so the missionaries likened the unknown to the known, and changed the verse to read: "Though your sins be as scarlet, they shall be as white as the meat of a coconut."

Under the circumstances, it would be hard to improve on that, wouldn't it?

At a Teachers' College, I once heard a lecturer on Alaska who failed, in many places, to be either clear or interesting because, unlike those African missionaries, he neglected to talk in terms of what his audience knew. He told us, for example, that Alaska had a gross area of 590,804 square miles, and a population of 64,356.

Half a million square miles—what does that mean to the average man? Precious little. He is not used to thinking in terms of square miles. They conjure up no mental picture. Suppose the speaker had said that the coastline of Alaska and its islands in longer than the distance around the globe, and that its area more than equals the combined areas of Vermont, New Hampshire, Maine, Massachusetts, Rhode Island, Connecticut, New York, New Jersey, Pennsylvania, Delaware, Maryland, West Virginia, North Carolina, South Carolina, Georgia, Florida, Mississippi and Tennessee. Would not that give everyone a fairly clear conception of the area of Alaska?

He said the population was 64,356. The chances are that not one person in ten remembered the census figures for five minutes—or even one minute. Why? Because the rapid saying of "sixty-four thousand, three hundred and fifty-six" does not make a very clear impression. It leaves only a loose, insecure impression, like words written on the sand of the seashore. The next wave of attention quite obliterates them. Would it not have been better to have stated the census in terms of something with which they were very familiar? Better still, why not talk about Alaska in terms of the very town where you are speaking?

In the following illustrations, which are the clearer, the (a) statement or the (b)?

a) Our nearest star is thirty-five trillion miles away.

b) A train going at the rate of a mile a minute would reach our nearest star in forty-eight million years; if a song were sung there and the sound could travel here it would be three million eight hundred thousand years before we could hear it. A spider's thread reaching to it would weigh five hundred tons.

c) St. Peter's, the biggest church in the world, is 232 yards long, and 364 feet wide.

d) It is about the size of two buildings like the capital at Washington piled on top of one another.

Sir Oliver Lodge happily uses this method when explaining the size and nature of atoms to a popular audience. I heard him tell a European audience that there were as many atoms in a drop of water as there were drops of water in the Mediterranean Sea; and many of his hearers had spent over a week sailing from Gibraltar to the Suez Canal. To bring the matter still closer home, he said there were as many atoms in one drop of water as there were blades of grass on all the earth.

Richard Harding Davis told a New York audience that the Mosque of St. Sophia was "about as big as the auditorium of the Fifth Avenue theatre". He said Brindisi "looks like Long Island City when you come into it from the rear."

Use this principle henceforth in your talks. If you are describing the great pyramid, first tell your hearers it is 451 feet, then tell them how high that is in terms of some building they see every day. Tell how many city blocks the base would cover. Don't speak about so many thousand gallons of this or so many hundred thousand barrels of that without also telling how many rooms the size of the one you are speaking in could be filled with that much liquid. Instead of saying twenty feet high, why not say one and a half times as high as this ceiling? Instead of talking about distance in terms of rods or miles, is it not clearer to say as far as from here to some station, or to such and such a street?

AVOID TECHNICAL TERMS

If you belong to a profession the work of which is technical—if you are a lawyer. A physician, an engineer, or are in a highly specialized line of business—be doubly careful when you talk to outsiders, to express yourself in plain terms and to give necessary details.

I say be doubly careful for, as a part of my professional duties. I have listened to hundreds of speeches that failed right at this point and failed woefully. The speakers appeared totally unconscious of the general public's widespread and profound ignorance regarding their particular specialties. So what happened? They rambled on and on, uttering thoughts, using phrases that fitted into their experience and were instantly and continuously meaningful to them; but to the uninitiated, they were about as clear as a river after the rains have fallen on the newly-ploughed cornfields along its banks.

What should such a speaker do? He ought to read and heed the following advice from the facile pen of ex-Senator Beveridge:

> It is a good practice to pick out the least intelligent looking person in the audience and strive to make that person interested in your argument. This can be done only by lucid statement of fact and clear reasoning. An even better method is to centre your talk on some small boy or girl present with presents.
>
> Say to yourself—say out loud to your audience, if you like—that you will try to be so plain that the child will understand and remember your explanation of the question discussed, and after the meeting be able to tell what you have said.

THE SECRET OF LINCOLN'S CLEARNESS

Lincoln had a deep and abiding affection for putting a proposition so that it would be instantly clear to everyone. In his first message to Congress, he used the phrase "sugar-coated". Mr. Defrees, the public printer, being Lincoln's personal friend, suggested to him that although the phrase might be all right for a stump speech in Illinois, it was not dignified enough for a historical state paper. "Well, Defrees," Lincoln replied, "if you think the time will ever come when the people will not understand what 'sugar-coated' means, I'll alter it; otherwise, I think I'll let it go."

He once explained to Dr. Gulliver, the President of Knox College, how he developed his "passion" for plain language, as he phrased it:

> Among my earliest recollections I remember how, when a mere child. I used to get irritated when anybody talked to me in a way I could not understand. I don't think I ever got angry at anything else in my life. But that always disturbed my temper, and has ever since. I can remember going to my little bedroom, after hearing the neighbours talk of an evening with my father, and spending no small part of the night walking up and down and trying to make out the exact meaning of some of their, to me, dark sayings. I could not sleep, though I often tried to, when I got on such a hunt after an idea, until I had caught it, and when I thought I had got it I was not satisfied until I had repeated it over and over, I until I had put it in language plain enough as I thought for and boy I knew comprehend. This was a kind of passion with me, and it has since stuck by me.

A passion? Yes, it must have amounted to that, for Mentor Graham, the schoolmaster of New Salem, testified: "I have known Lincoln to study for hours the best way of three to express an idea."

An all too common reason why men fail to be intelligible is this: the thing they wish to express is not clear even to themselves. Hazy impressions! Indistinct, vague ideas! The result? Their minds work no better in a mental fog than a camera does in a physical fog. They need to be as disturbed over obscurity and ambiguity as Lincoln was. They need to use his methods.

APPEAL TO THE SENSE OF SIGHT

The nerves that lead from the eye to the brain are many times larger than those leading from the ear; and science tells us that we give twenty-five times as much attention to eye suggestions as we do to ear suggestions.

"One seeing," says an old Japanese proverb, "is better than a hundred times telling about."

So, if you wish to be clear, picture your points, visualize your ideas. That was the plan of the late John H. Patterson, President of the well-known National Cash Register Company. He wrote an article for *System Magazine,* outlining the methods he used in speaking to his workmen and his sales forces:

> I hold that one cannot rely on speech alone to make himself understood or to gain and hold attention. A dramatic supplement is needed. It is better to supplement whenever possible with pictures which show the right and the wrong way; diagrams are more convincing than mere words, and pictures are more convincing than diagrams. The ideal presentation of a subject is one in which every sub-division is pictured and in which the words are used only to connect them. I early found that in dealing with men, a picture was worth more than anything I could say.
>
> Little grotesque drawings are wonderfully effective.... I have a whole system of cartooning or "chart talks". A circle with a dollar mark means a piece of money, a bag marked with a dollar is a lot of money. Many good effects can be had with moon faces. Draw a circle, put in a few dashes for the eyes, nose, mouth, and ears, Twisting these lines gives the expressions. The out-of-date man has the corner of his mouth down; the chipper, up-to-date fellow has the curves up. The drawings are homely, but the most effective cartoonists are not the men who make the prettiest pictures; the thing is to express the idea and the contrast.
>
> The big bag and the little bag of money, side by side, are the natural heads for the right way as opposed to the wrong way; the one brings much money, the other little money. If you sketch these rapidly as you talk, there is no danger of people's letting their minds wander; they are bound to look at what you are doing and thus to go with you through the successive stages to the point you want to make. And again, the funny figures put people in good humour.

I used to employ an artist to hand around in the shops with me and quietly make sketches of things that were not being done right. Then the sketches were made into drawings and I called the men together and showed them exactly what they were doing. When I heard of the stereopticon I immediately bought one and projected the drawings on the screen, which, of course, made them even more effective than on paper. Then came the moving picture. I think that I had one of the first machines ever made and now we have a big department with many motion picture films and more than 60,000 coloured stereopticon slides.

Not every subject or occasion, of course, lends itself to exhibits and drawings; but let us use them when we can. They attract attention, stimulate interest and often make our meaning doubly clear.

ROCKEFELLER RAKING OFF THE COINS

Mr. Rockefeller also used the columns of *System Magazine* to tell how he appealed to the sense of sight to make clear the financial situation of the Colorado Fuel and Iron Company:

I found that they (the employees of the Colorado Fuel and Iron Co.) imagined the Rockefellers had been drawing immense profits from their interests in Colorado; no end of people had told them so. I explained the exact situation to them. I showed them that during the fourteen years in which we had been connected with the Colorado Fuel and Iron Co., it had never paid one cent in dividends upon the common stock.

At one of our meetings, I gave a practical illustration of the finances of the company. I put a number of coins on the table. I swept off a portion which represented their wages—for the first claim upon the company is the payroll. Then I took away more coins to represent the salaries of the officers, and then the remaining coins to represent the fees of the directors. There were no coins left for the stockholders. And when I asked: "Men, is it fair, in this corporation where we are all partners, that three of the partners should get all the earnings, be they large or small—all of them—and the fourth nothing?"

After the illustration, one of the men made a speech for higher wages. I asked him, "Is it fair for you to want more wages when one of the partners gets nothing?" He admitted that it did not look like a square deal; I heard no more about increasing the wages.

Make your eye appeals definite and specific. Paint mental pictures that stand out as sharp and clear as a stag's horn silhouetted against the setting sun. For example, the word "dog" calls up a more or less definite picture of such an animal—perhaps a cocker spaniel, a Scotch terrier, a St. Bernard, or a Pomeranian. Notice how much more distinct an image springs into your mind when I say "bulldog"—the term is less inclusive. Doesn't "a brindle bulldog call up a still inclusive. Doesn't "a brindle bulldog" call up a still more explicit picture? Is it not more vivid to say "a black Shetland pony" than to talk of "a horse"? Doesn't "a white bantam rooster with a broken leg" give a much more definite and sharp picture them merely the word "fowl"?

RESTATE YOUR IMPORTANT IDEAS IN DIFFERENT WORDS

Napoleon declared repetition to be the only serious principle of rhetoric. He knew that because an idea which was clear to him was not always proof that it was instantly grasped by others. He knew that it takes time to comprehend new ideas, that the mind must be kept focussed on them. In short, he knew they must be repeated. Not in exactly the same language. People will rebel at that, and rightly so. But if the repetition is couched in fresh phraseology, if it is varied, your hearers will never regard it as repetition at all.

Let us take a specific example. The late Mr. Bryan said: "You cannot make people understand a subject, unless you understand that subject yourself. The more clearly you have a subject in mind, the more clearly can you present that subject to the minds of others."

The last sentence here is merely a restatement of the idea contained in the first, but when these sentences are spoken, the mind does not have time to see that it is repetition. It only *feels* that the subject has been made more clear.

I seldom teach a single session of this course without hearing one or perhaps half a dozen talks that would have been more clear, more impressive, had the speaker but employed this principle of restatement. It is almost entirely ignored by the beginner. And what a pity!

USE GENERAL ILLUSTRATIONS AND SPECIFIC INSTANCES

One of the surest and easiest ways to make your points clear is to follow them with general illustrations and concrete cases. What is the difference between the two? One, as the term implies, is general; the other, specific.

Let us illustrate the difference between them and the uses of each with a concrete example. Suppose we take the statement "There are professional men and women who earn astonishingly large incomes."

Is that statement very clear? Have you a clearcut idea of what the speaker really means? No, and the speaker himself cannot be sure of what such an assertion will call up in the minds of others. It may cause the country doctor to think of a family doctor in a small city with an income of five thousand. It may cause a successful mining engineer to think in terms of the men in his profession who make a hundred thousand a year. The statement, as it stands, is entirely too vague and loose. It needs to be tightened. A few illuminating details ought to be given to indicate what profession the speaker refers to and what he means by "astonishingly large".

"There are lawyers, prize-fighters, song-writers, novelists, playwrights, painters, actors and singers who make more than the President of the United States."

Now, hasn't one a much clearer idea of what the speaker meant? However, he has not individualized. He has used general illustrations, not specific instances. He has said "singers", not Rosa Ponselle, Kirsten Flagstad, or Lily Pons.

So the statement is still more or less vague. We cannot call up concrete cases to illustrate it. Should not the speaker do it for us? Would he not be clearer if he employed specific examples—as is done in the following paragraph:

The great trial lawyers Samuel Untermeyer and Max Steuer earn as much as one million dollars a year. Jack Dempsey's annual has been known to be as high as a half-million dollars. Joe Louis, the young, uneducated negro pugilist, while still in his twenties, has earned more than a half-million dollars. Irving Berlin's rag-time music is reported to have brought him a half million dollars yearly. Sidney Kingsley has made ten thousand dollars a week royalty on his plays. H.G. Wells has admitted, in his autobiography, that his pen has brought him three million dollars. Diego Rivera has earned, from his paintings, more than half a million dollars in a year. Katherine Cornell has repeatedly refused five thousand dollars a week to go into pictures. Lawrence Tibbet and Grace Moore are reported to have an annual income of a quarter-million dollars.

Now, has not one an extremely plain and vivid idea of exactly and precisely what the speaker wanted to convey?

Be concrete. Be definite. Be specific. This quality of definiteness not only makes for clearness but for impressiveness and conviction and interest also.

DO NOT EMULATE THE MOUNTAIN GOAT

Professor William James, in one of his talks to teachers, pauses to remark that one can make only one point in a lecture, and the lecture he referred to lasted an hour. Yet I recently heard a speaker, who was limited by a stopwatch to three minutes, begin by saying that he wanted to call our attention to eleven points. Sixteen and a half seconds to each phase of his subject! Seems incredible, doesn't it, that an intelligent man should attempt anything so manifestly absurd. True, I am quoting an extreme case, but the tendency to err in that fashion, if not to that degree, handicaps almost every novice. He is like a Cook's guide who shows Paris to the tourist in one day. It can be done, just as one can walk through the Museum of Natural History in thirty minutes. But neither clearness nor enjoyment results. Many a talk fails to be clear because the speaker seems intent upon establishing a world's record for ground covered in the allotted time. He leaps from one point to another with the swiftness and agility of a mountain goat.

The talks in this course must, owing to the pressure of time, be short; so cute your cloth accordingly. If, for example, you are to speak on Labour Unions, do not attempt to tell us in three or six minutes why they came into existence, the methods they employ, the good they have accomplished, the evil they have wrought, and how to solve industrial disputes. No, no; if you strive to do that, no one will have a very clear conception of what you have said. It will be all confused, a blur, too sketchy, too much of a mere outline.

Wouldn't it be the part of wisdom to take one phase and one phase only of labour unions, and cover that adequately and illustrate it? It would. That kind of speech leaves a single impression. It is lucid, easy to listen to, easy to remember.

However, if you must cover several phases of your topic, it is often advisable to summarize briefly at the end. Let us see how that suggestion operates. Here is a summary of this lesson. Does the reading of it help to make the message we have been presenting more lucid, more comprehensible?

"One picture is worth ten thousand words."

—Chinese Proverb

"Clarity of mind means clarity of passion, too; this is why a great and clear mind loves ardently and sees distinctly what he loves."

—Blaise Pascal

....

Improving Your Diction

"Be impeccable with your word. Speak with integrity. Say only what you mean. Avoid using the word to speak against yourself or to gossip about others. Use the power of your word in the direction of truth and love."

—Don Miguel Ruiz

A short time ago an Englishman, without employment and without financial reserves, was walking the streets seeking a position. He entered the office of Mr. Paul Gibbons, a well-known businessman, and asked for an interview. Mr. Gibbons looked at the stranger distrustfully. His appearance was emphatically against him. His clothes were shabby and threadbare, and over all of him were written large the unmistakable signs of financial distress. Half out of curiosity half out of pity Mr. Gibbons granted the interview. At first, he had intended to listen for only a moment, but the moments grew into minutes, and the minutes mounted into an hour; and the conversation still continued. It ended by Mr. Gibbons telephoning Mr. Roland Taylor, the manager of a well-known firm of stockbrokers; and Mr. Taylor, one of the leading financiers of that city, invited this stranger to lunch and secured for him a desirable position, how was this man, with the air and outward appearance of failure, able to effect such a prized connection within so short a time?

The secret can be divulged in a single phrase: his command of the English language. He was, in reality, an Oxford man who had come to town on business mission which had ended in disaster, leaving him stranded, without funds and without friends. But he spoke his mother tongue with such precision and beauty that his listeners soon forgot his rusty shoes, his frayed coat, his unshaven face. His diction became an immediate passport into the best business circles.

This man's story is somewhat extraordinary, but it illustrates a broad and fundamental truth, namely, that we are judged each day by our speech. Our words reveal our refinements; they tell the discerning listener of the company we have kept; they are the hallmarks of education and culture.

We have only four contacts with the world, you and I. We are evaluated and classified by four things: by what we do, by how we look, by what we say, and by how we say it. Yet many a man blunders through a long life time, after he leaves school, without any conscious effort to enrich his stock of words, to master their shades of meaning, to speak with precision and distinction. He comes habitually to use the overworked and exhausted phrases of the office and street. Small wonder that his talk lacks distinction and individuality. Small wonder that he often violets the accepted traditions of pronunciation, and that he sometimes transgresses the very canons of English grammar itself. I have heard even college graduates say "ain't", and "he don't", "between you and I". And if men with academic degrees gracing their names commit such errors, what can we expect of those whose education has been cut short by the pressure of economic necessity?

Years ago, I stood one afternoon day-dreaming in the Colosseum at Rome. A stranger approached me, and English colonial. He introduced himself, and began talking of his experiences in the Eternal City. He had not spoken three minutes until he had said "you was", and "I done". That morning, when he arose, he had polished his shoes and put on spotless linen in order to maintain his own self-respect and to win the respect of those with whom he came in contact, but he had made no attempt whatever to polish his phrases and to speak spotless sentences. He would have been ashamed, for example, of not raising his hat to a woman when he spoke, but he was not ashamed—no, he was not even conscious—of violating the usages of grammar, of offending the ears of discriminating auditors. By his own words, he stood revealed and placed and classified.

His woeful use of the English language proclaimed to the world continually and unmistakably that he was not a person of culture.

Dr. Charles W. Eliot, after he had been President of Harvard for a third of a century, declared: "I recognize but one mental acquisition as a necessary part of the education of a lady or gentleman, namely, and accurate and refined use of the mother tongue." This is significant pronouncement. Ponder over it.

But how, you ask, are we to become intimate with words, to speak them with beauty and accuracy? Fortunately, there is no mystery about the means to be employed, no legerdemain. The method is an open secret. Lincoln used it with amazing success. No other American ever wove words into such comely patterns, or produced with prose such matchless music: "with malice towards none, with charity for all." Was Lincoln, whose father was a shiftless, illiterate carpenter and whose mother was a woman of no extraordinary attainments—was he endowed by nature with this gift for words? There is no evidence to support such an assumption. When he was elected to Congress, he described his education in the official records at Washington, with one adjective: "defective". He had attended school less than twelve months in his entire life. And who had been his mentors? Zachariah Birney and Caleb Hazel in the forests of Kentucky, Azel Dorsey and Andrew Crawford along Pigeon Creek in Indiana—itinerant pedagogues, all of them, drifting from one pioneer settlement to another, eking out an existence wherever a few scholars could be found who were willing to exchange hams and maize and wheat for the three Rs. Lincoln had meagre assistance, little of uplift or inspiration from them and little, too, from his daily environment.

The farmers and merchants, the lawyers and litigants with whom he associated in the Eighth Judicial District of Illinois, possessed no magic with words. But Lincoln did not—and this is the significant fact to remember—Lincoln did not squander all his time with his mental equals and inferiors. He made boon companions out of the elite minds, the singers, the poets of the ages. He could repeat from memory whole pages of Burns and Byron and Browning. He wrote a lecture on Burns. He had one copy Byron's poems for his office and another for his home. The office copy had been used so much that it fell open, whenever it was lifted, to

Don Juan. Even when he was in the White House and the tragic burdens of the Civil War were sapping his strength and etching deep furrows in his face, he often found time to take a copy of Hood's poems to bed. Sometimes he awoke in the middle of the night and, opening the book, he chanced upon verses that especially stirred or pleased. Getting up, clad only in his night-shirt and slippers, he stole through the halls until he found his secretary and read to him poem after poem. In the White House, he found time to repeat long, memorized passages from Shakespeare, to criticize the actor's reading of them, to give his own individual interpretation. "I have gone over some of Shakespeare's plays," he wrote to Hackett, the actor, "perhaps as frequently as any unprofessional reader. *Lear, Richard III, Henry VIII, Hamlet,* and especially *Macbeth.* I think nothing equals *Macbeth.* It is wonderful!"

Lincoln was devoted to verse. Not only did lie memorize and repeat it, both in private and public, but he even essayed to write it. He read one of his long poems at his sister's wedding. Later, in middle life, he filled a notebook with his original compositions, but he was so shy about these creations that he never permitted even his closest friends to read them.

"This self-educated man," writes Robinson in his book *Lincoln as a Man of Letters,* "clothed his mind with the materials of genuine culture. Call it genius or talent, the process of his attainment was that described by Professor Emerton in speaking of the education of Erasmus: 'He was no longer at school, but was simply educating himself by the only pedagogical method which ever yet produced any results anywhere, namely, by the method of his own tireless energy in continuous study and practice'."

This awkward pioneer, who used to shuck Indian corn and butcher hogs for thirty-one cents a day on the Pigeon Creek farms of Indiana, delivered, at Gettysburg, one of the most beautiful addresses ever spoken by mortal man. One hundred and seventy thousand men fought there. Seven thousand were killed. Yet Charles Sumner said, shortly after Lincoln's death, that Lincoln's address would live when the memory of the battle was lost, and that the battle would one day be remembered largely because of the speech. Who will doubt the correctness of this prophecy? Isn't it, even in this generation, beginning to be fulfilled? Do you not, even now, think of the speech as much as of the fighting when you hear the name "Gettysburg"?

Edward Everett spoke for two hours at Gettysburg; all that he said has long since been forgotten. Lincoln spoke for less than two minutes: a photographer attempted to take his picture while delivering the speech, but Lincoln had finished before the primitive camera could be set up and focused.

Lincoln's address has been cast in imperishable bronze and placed in a library at Oxford as an example of what can be done with the English language. It ought to be memorized by every student of public speaking.

> Four score and seven years ago our fathers brought forth on this continent a new nation, conceived in liberty, and dedicated to the proposition that all men are created equal. Now we are engaged in a great civil war testing whether that nation, or any nation so conceived and so dedicated can long endure. We are met on a great battlefield of that war. We have come to dedicate a portion of that field as a final resting-place for those who here gave their lives that that nation might live. It is altogether fitting and proper that we should do this. But in a larger sense we cannot dedicate, we cannot consecrate, we cannot allow this ground. The brave men, living and dead, who struggled here, have consecrated it, far above our poor power to add or detract. The world will little note, nor long remember, what we say here, but it can never forget what they did here. It is for us, the living, rather to be dedicated here to the unfinished work which they who fought here have thus far so nobly advanced. It is rather for us to be here dedicated to the great task remaining before us, that from these honoured dead we take increased devotion to that cause for which they gave the last full measure of devotion; that we here highly resolve that these dead shall not have died in vain; that this nation, under God, shall have a new birth of freedom; and that government of the people, by the people, for the people, shall not perish from the earth.

It is commonly supposed that Lincoln originated the immortal phrase which closed this address; but did he? Herndon, his law partner, had given

Lincoln, several years previously. A copy of Theodore Parker's addresses. Lincoln read and underscored in this book the words "Democracy is direct self-government, over all the people, by all the people, and for all the people". Theodore Parker may have borrowed his phraseology from Webster who had said, four years earlier, in his famous reply to Hayne: "The people's government, made for the people, made by the people, and answerable to the people." Webster may have borrowed his phraseology from President James Monroe who had given voice to the same idea a third of a century earlier. And to whom was James Monroe indebted? Five hundred years before Monroe was born, Wyclif had said, in the preface to the translation of the Scriptures, that "this Bible is for the government of the people, by the people, and for the people". And long before Wycliffe lived, more than 400 years before the birth of Christ, Cleon, in an address to the men of Athens, spoke of a ruler "of the people, by the people, and for the people". And from what ancient source Cleon drew his inspiration, is a matter lost in the fog and night of antiquity.

How little there is that is new! How much even the great speakers owe to their reading and to their association with books!

Books! There is the secret! He who would enrich and enlarge his stock of words must soak and tan his mind constantly in the vats of literature. "The only lamentation that I always feel in the presence of a library", said John Bright, "is that life is too short and I have no hope of a full enjoyment of the ample repast spread before me". Bright left school at fifteen, and went to work in a cotton mill, and he never had the chance of schooling again. Yet he became one of the most brilliant speakers of the generation, famous for his superb command of the English language. He read and studied and copied in notebooks and committed to memory long passages from the poetry of Byron and Milton, and Wordsworth, and Shakespeare and Shelley. He went through *Paradise Lost* each year to enrich his stock of words.

Charles James Fox read Shakespeare aloud to improve his style. Gladstone called his study a "Temple of Peace", and in it he kept 15,000 books. He was helped most, he confessed, by reading the works of St. Augustine, Bishop Butler, Dante, Aristotle, and Homer. *The Iliad* and

The Odyssey enthralled him. He wrote six books on Homeric poetry and Homeric times.

The younger Pitt's practise was to look over a page or two of Greek or Latin and then to translate the passage into his own language. He did this daily for ten years, and "he acquired an almost unrivalled power of putting his thoughts, without pre-meditation, into words well selected and well arranged."

Demosthenes copied Thucydides' history eight times in his own handwriting in order that he might acquire the majestic and impressive phraseology of that famous historian. The result? Two thousand years later, in order to improve his style, Woodrow Wilson studied works of Demosthenes. Mr. Asquith found his best training in reading the works of Bishop Berkeley.

Tennyson studied the Bible daily. Tolstoy read and re-read the Gospels until he knew long passages by memory. Ruskin's mother forced him by steady, daily toil to memorize long chapters of the Bible and to read the entire Book through aloud each year, "every syllable, hard names and all, from Genesis to the Apocalypse." To that discipline and study Ruskin attributed his taste and style in literature.

R.L.S. are said to be the best-loved initials in the English language. Robert Louis Stevenson was essentially a writer's writer. How did he develop the charming style that made him famous? Fortunately, he has told us the story himself.

Whenever I read a book or a passage that particularly pleased me, in which a thing was said or an effect rendered with propriety, in which there was either some conspicuous force or some happy distinction in the style, I must sit down at once and set myself to ape that quality. I was unsuccessful, and I knew it; and tried again, and was again unsuccessful, and always unsuccessful; but at least in these vain bouts I got some practice in rhythm, in harmony, in construction, and coordination of parts.

I have thus played the sedulous ape to Hazlitt, to Lamb, to Wordsworth, to Sir Thomas Browne, to Defoe, to Hawthorne, to Montaigne.

That like it or not, is the way to learn to write; whether I have profited or not, that is the way. It was the way Keats learned, and there never was a finer temperament for literature than Keats'.

It is the great point of these imitations that there still shines beyond the student's reach, his inimitable model. Let him try as he please, he is still sure of failure; and it is an old and very true saying that failure is the only high-road to success.

Enough of names and specific stories. The secret is out. Lincoln wrote it to a young man eager to become a successful lawyer: "It is only to get the books and to read and study them carefully. Work, work, work is the main thing."

What books? Begin with Arnold Bennett's *How to Live on Twenty-four Hours a Day.* This book will be as stimulating as a cold bath. It will tell you a lot about that most interesting of all subjects—yourself. It will reveal to you how much time you are wasting each day, how to stop the wastage, and how to utilize what you salvage. The entire book has only 103 pages. You can get through it easily in a week. Tear out twenty pages each morning, put them in your hip pocket. Then offer up upon the altar of the morning newspaper only ten minutes instead of the customary twenty or thirty minutes.

"I have given up newspapers in exchange for Tacitus and Thucydides, for Newton and Euclid," wrote Thomas Jefferson, "and I find myself much the happier." Don't you believe that you, by following Jefferson's example at least to the extent of cutting your newspaper reading in half, would find yourself happier and wiser as the weeks go by? Aren't you, at any rate, willing to try it for a month, and to devote the time you have thus salvaged to the more enduring value of a good book? Why not read the pages you are to carry with you while waiting for lifts, for buses, for food, for appointments?

After you have read those twenty pages, replace them in the book, tear out another twenty. When you have consumed them all, put a rubber band around the covers to hold the loose pages in place. Isn't it better far to have a book butchered and mutilated in that fashion, with its message in your head, than to have it reposing unbruised and unread upon the shelves of your library?

After you have finished *How to live on Twenty-four Hours a Day*, you may be interested in another book by the same author. Try *The Human Machine*. This book will enable you to handle people more tactfully, it will develop your poise and self-possession. These books are recommended here not only for what they say, but for the way they say it, for the enriching and refining effect they are sure to have upon your vocabulary.

Some other books that will be helpful are suggested: *The Octopus* and *The Pit* by Frank Norris are two of the best American novels ever written. The first deals with turmoils and human tragedies occurring in the wheat fields of California; the second portrays the battles of the bears and bulls on the Chicago Board of Trade. *Tess of the D'Urbervilles* by Thomas Hardy is one of the most beautiful tales ever written. *A Man's Value to Society* by Newell Dwight Hillis and Professor William James' *Talks to Teachers* are two books well worth reading. *Ariel, A Life of Shelley,* by Andre Maurois, Byron's *Childe Harold's Pilgrimage* and Robert Louis Stevenson's *Travels with a Donkey* should also be on your list.

Make Ralph Waldo Emerson your daily companion. Command him to give you first his famous essay on self-Reliance. Let him whisper into your ear marching sentences like these:

Speak your latent conviction, and it shall be the universal sense; for always the inmost becomes the outmost—and our first thought is rendered back to us by the trumpets of the Last Judgment. Familiar as the voice of the mind is to each, the highest merit we ascribe to Moses, Plato, and Milton, is that they set at naught books and traditions, and spoke not what men said but what they thought. A man should learn to detect and watch that gleam of light which flashes across his mind from within, more than the lustre of the firmament of bards and sages. Yet he dismisses without notice his thought, because it is his. In every work of genius we recognize our own rejected thoughts: they come back to us with a certain alienated majesty. Great works of art have no more affecting lesson for us than this. They teach us to abide by our spontaneous impression with good-humoured inflexibility then most when the whole cry of voice is on the other side. Else, tomorrow a stranger will say with masterly good sense precisely what we have thought and felt all the time, and we shall be forced to take with shame our own opinion from another.

There is a time in every man's education when he arrives at the conviction that envy is ignorance; that imitation is suicide; that he must take himself for better, for worse, as his portion; that though the wide universe is full of good, no kernel of nourishing corn can come to him but through his toil bestowed on that plot of ground which is given to him to till. The power which resides in him is new in nature, and none but he knows what that is which he can do, nor does he know until he has tried.

But we have really left the best authors to the last. What are they? When Sir Henry Irving was asked to furnish a list of what he regarded as the hundred best books, he replied: "Before a hundred books, commend me to the study of two—the Bible and Shakespeare." Sir Henry was right. Drink from these two great fountain sources of English literature. Drink long and often. Toss your evening newspaper aside and say, "Shakespeare, come here and talk to me tonight of Romeo and his Juliet, of Macbeth and his ambition."

If you do these things, what will be your reward? Gradually, unconsciously but inevitably, your diction will begin to take on added beauty and refinement. Gradually, you will begin to reflect somewhat the glory and beauty and majesty of your companions. "Tell me what you read," observed Goethe, "and I will tell you what you are."

This reading programme that I have suggested will require little but willpower, little but a more careful husbanding of time…. You can purchase pocket copies of Emerson's essays and Shakespeare's plays for a few pence each.

THE SECRET OF MARK TWAIN'S WAY WITH WORDS

How did Mark Twain develop his delightful facility with words? As a young man, he travelled all the way from Missouri to Nevada by the ponderously slow and really painful stage coach. Food—and sometimes even water— had to be carried for both passengers and horses. Extra weight might have meant the difference between safety and disaster; baggage was charged for by the ounce, and yet Mark Twain carried with him a Webster's Unabridged Dictionary over mountain passes, across scorched deserts, and through a land infested with bandits and Indians. He wanted to make himself master of words, and with his characteristic courage and common sense, he set about doing the things necessary to bring that mastery about.

Both William Pitt and his father, Lord Chatham, studied the dictionary twice, every page, every word of it. Browning pored over it daily, finding in it entertainment as well as instruction. Lincoln "would sit in the twilight", records his biographers, Nicolay and Hay, "and read a dictionary as long as he could see". These are not exceptional instances. Every writer and speaker of distinction has done the same.

Woodrow Wilson was superbly skilful with the English language. Some of his writings—parts of his Declaration of War against Germany—will undoubtedly take a place in literature. Here is his own story of how he learned to marshal words:

> My father never allowed any member of his household to use an incorrect expression. Any slip on the part of one of the children was at once corrected; any unfamiliar word was immediately explained; each of us was encouraged to find a use for it in our conversation so as to fix it in our memories.

A speaker who is often complimented upon the firm texture of his sentences and the simple beauty of his language, during the course of a conversation recently, lifted the embargo on the secret of his power to choose true and incisive words. Each time he discovers an unfamiliar word in conversation or reading matter, he notes it in his memorandum book. Then, just prior to retiring at night, he consults his dictionary and makes the word his own. If he has gathered no material in this fashion during the day, he studies a page or two of Fernald's *Synonyms, Antonyms and Prepositions,* noting the exact meaning of the words which he would ordinarily interchange as perfect synonyms. A new word a day—that is his motto. This means in the course of a year three hundred and sixty-five additional tools for expression. These new words are stored away in a small pocket notebook, and their meanings reviewed at odd moments during the day.

He has found that a word becomes a permanent acquisition to his vocabulary when he has used it three times.

ROMANTIC STORIES BEHIND THE WORDS YOU USE

Use a dictionary not only to ascertain the meaning of the word, but also to find its derivation. Its history, its origin is usually set down in brackets after the definition. Do not imagine for a moment that the words you speak each day are only dull, listless sounds, they are reeking with colour, they are alive with romance. You cannot, for example, say so prosaic a thing as, "Telephone the grocer for sugar", without using words that we have borrowed from many different language and civilizations. *Telephone* is made from two Greek words, *tele,* meaning far, and *phone,* meaning sound. *Grocer* comes from an old French word, *grossier,* and the French came from the Latin, *grossarius;* it literally means one who sells by the wholesale or gross. We got our word *sugar* from the French; the French borrowed it from the Spanish; the Spanish lifted it from the Arabic; the Arabic took it from the Persian; and the Persian word *shaker* was derived from the Sanskrit *carkara,* meaning candy.

You may work for or own a *company. Company* is derived from an old French word meaning *companion;* and *companion* is literally *com,* with, and *panis,* bread. Your *companion* is one with whom you have bread. A *company* is really an association of people who are trying to make their bread together. Your *salary* literally means your *salt* money. The Roman soldiers drew a certain allowance for salt, and one day some wag spoke of his entire income as his *salarium,* and created a bit of slang which his long since become respectable English. You are holding in your hand a *book.* It literally means *beech,* for a long time ago the Anglo-Saxons scratched their words on *beech* trees and on tablets of *beech* wood. A *dollar* literally means *valley. Dollars* were first coined in St. Joachim's *Thaler* or *dale* or *valley* in the sixteenth century.

The words *janitor* and *January* have both come down from the name of an Etruscan blacksmith who lived in Rome and made a specialty of locks and bolts for doors. When he died, he was deified as a pagan god, and was represented as having two faces, so that he could look both ways at the same time, and was associated with the opening and closing of doors. So the month that stood at the close of one year and the opening of another was called *January,* or the month of *Janus.* So when we talk of *January* or a *Janitor,* a keeper of doors, we are honouring the name of a blacksmith who lived a thousand years before the birth of Christ and who had a wife by the name of Jane.

The seventh month, *July,* was named after Julius Caesar; so the Emperor Augustus, not to be outdone, called the next month *August.* But the eighth month had only thirty days at that time, and Augustus did not propose to have the month named after him any shorter than a month named after Julius; so he took one day away from February and added it to August, and the marks of this vain-glorious theft are evident on the calendar hanging in your home today. Truly, you will find the history of words fascinating.

Please look up in a large dictionary the derivation of these words: atlas, boycott, cereal, colossal, concord curfew, education, finance, lunatic, panic, palace, pecuniary, sandwich, tantalize. Get the stories behind them. It will make them doubly colourful, doubly interesting. You will use them, then, with added zest and pleasure.

REWRITING ONE SENTENCE A HUNDRED AND FOUR TIMES

Strive to say precisely what you mean, to express the most delicate nuances of thought. That is not always easy—not even for experienced writers. Fanny Hurst told me that she sometimes rewrote her sentences from fifty to a hundred times. Only a few days prior to the conversation she said she had rewritten one sentence one hundred and four times by actual count. Yet she was so accomplished a writer that the magazines were paying her four hundred pounds a story. Mabel Herbert Urner confided to me that she sometimes spent an entire afternoon eliminating only one or two sentences from a short story that was to be syndicated through the newspapers.

Gouverneur Morris has told how Richard Harding Davis laboured incessantly for just the right word:

Every phrase in his fiction was, of all the myriad phrases he could think of, the fittest in his relentless judgment to survive. Phrases, paragraphs, pages, whole stories even, were written over and over again. He worked upon a principle of elimination. If he wished to describe an automobile turning in at a gate, he made first a long and elaborate description from which there was omitted no detail, which the most observant pair of eyes in Christendom has ever noted with reference to just such a turning. Thereupon he would begin a process of omitting one by one those details which he had been at such pains to recall; and after each omission he would ask himself, 'Does the picture remain?' If it did not, he restored the detail which he had just omitted, and experimented with the sacrifice of some other, and so on, and so on, until after Herculean labour there remained for the reader one of those swiftly flashed ice-clear pictures (complete in every detail) with which his tales and romances are so delightfully and continuously adorned.

Most students of this course have neither time nor disposition to search as diligently for words as the author just described. These instances are cited to show you the importance successful writers attach to proper diction and expression, in the hope that it may encourage students to take an increased interest in the use of English. It is, of course, not practical for a speaker to hesitate in a sentence and *uh-uh* about, hunting for the word which will exactly express the shade of meaning he desires to convey, but he should practise preciseness of expression in his daily intercourse until it comes unconsciously. He should, but does he? He does not.

Milton is reported to have employed eight thousand words. And Shakespeare fifteen thousand. A standard dictionary contains fifty thousand less than half a million; but the average man, according to popular estimates, gets along with approximately two thousand. He has some verbs, enough connectives to stick them together, a handful of nouns, and a few overworked adjectives. He is too lazy, mentally, or to absorbed in business, to train for precision and exactness. The result? Let me give you an illustration. I once spent a few unforgettable days on the rim of the Grand Canyon of Colorado. In the course of an afternoon, I heard a lady apply the same adjective to a Chow dog, an orchestral selection, a man's disposition, and the Grand Canyon itself. They were all "beautiful".

What should she have said? Here are the synonyms that Roget lists for *beautiful*. Which adjectives do you think she should have employed?

Adjective: *beautiful,* beauteous, handsome, pretty, lovely, graceful, elegant, exquisite, delicate, dainty.

comely, fair, goodly, bonny good-looking, well-favoured, well-informed, well-proportioned, shapely, symmetrical, harmonious.

bright, bright-eyed, rosy-cheeked, rosy, ruddy, blooming, in full bloom.

trim, trig, tidy, neat, spruce, smart, jaunty, dapper.

brilliant, shining, sparkling, radiant, splendid, resplendent, dazzling, glowing, glossy, sleek, rich, gorgeous, superb, magnificent, grand, fine.

artistic, aesthetic, picturesque, pictorial, enchanting, attractive, becoming, ornamental.

perfect, unspotted, spotless, immaculate, undeformed, undefaced.

passable, presentable, tolerable, not amiss

The synonyms just quoted have been taken from Roget's *Treasury of Words*. It is an abridged edition of Roget's *Thesaurus*. What a help this book is! Personally, I never write without having it at my elbow. I find occasion to use it ten times as often as I use the dictionary.

What years of toil Roget consecrated to its making; yet it will come and sit on your desk and serve you a lifetime for the price of an inexpensive necktie. It is not a book to be stored away on a library shelf. It is a tool to be used constantly. Use it when writing out and polishing the diction of your talks. Use it in dictating your letters and your business reports. Use it daily, and it will double and treble your power with words.

SHUN WORN-OUT PHRASES

Strive not only to be exact, but to be fresh and original. Have the courage to say the thing as you see it, for "the God of things as they are". For example, shortly after the flood, some original mind first used the comparison, "cool as a cucumber". It was extraordinarily good then because it was extraordinarily fresh. Even as late as Belshazzar's famous feast, it may still have retained enough of its pristine vigour to warrant its use in an after-dinner speech. But what man who prides himself on his originality would be guilty of repeating it at this somewhat late date?

Here are a dozen similes to express coldness. Aren't they just as effective as the hackneyed "cucumber" comparison, and far fresher and more acceptable?

Cold as a frog.

Cold as a hot-water bag in the morning.

Cold as a ramrod.

Cold as a tomb.

Cold as Greenland's icy mountains.

Cold as clay—*Coleridge*

Cold as a turtle—*Richard Cumberland*

Cauld as the drifting snow—*Allan Cunningham*

Cold as salt—*James Huneker*

Cold as an earthworm—*Maurice Maeterlinck*

Cold as dawn.

Cold as rain in autumn.

While the mood is upon you, think now of similes of your own to convey the idea of coldness. Have the courage to be distinctive. Write them here:

Cold as . . . .

Cold as . . . .

Cold as . . . .

Cold as . . . .

Cold as . . . .

I once asked Kathleen Norris, who is reputed to be the highest-paid writer of magazine serial fiction, how style could be developed. "By reading classics of prose and poetry," she replied, "and by critically eliminating stock phrases, and hackneyed expressions from your work.'

A magazine editor once told me that when he found two or three hackneyed expressions in a story submitted for publication, he returned it to the author without wasting time reading it; for, he added, one who has no originality of expression will exhibit little originality of thought.

> *"Ten people who speak make more noise than*
> *ten thousand who are silent."*
>
> **—Napoleon Bonaparte**

> *"Soak yourself full of the world's best literature so that you will*
> *have words, strong words, clear words, for your speaking."*
>
> **—Dr. Lynn Harold Hough**

CHAPTER 12

....

How to Interest Your Audience

"I believe in anything that will engage the audience
and make the story more effective."

—J.J. Abrams

If you were invited to dine at the home of a rich man in certain sections of China, it would be proper to toss chicken bones and olive seeds over your shoulder on to the floor. You pay your host a compliment when you do that. You show that you realize that he is wealthy, that he has plenty of servants to tidy up after the meal. And he likes it.

You can be reckless with the remains of your sumptuous meal in a rich man's home, but in some parts of China the poorer people must save even the water they bathe in. To heat water costs so much that they must buy it at a hot-water shop. After they have bathed in it, they can take it back and sell it secondhand to the shopkeeper from whom they purchased it. When the second customer has soiled it, the water still retains a market value, although the price has softened a bit.

Have you found these facts about Chinese life interesting? If so, do you know why? Because those are very unusual aspects of very usual things. They are strange truths about such commonplace events as dining out and bathing.

That is what interests us—something new about the old.

Let us take another illustration. This page you are reading now, this sheet of paper you are looking at—it is very ordinary, isn't it? You have seen countless thousands of such pages. It seems dull and insipid now; but if I tell you a strange fact about it, you are almost sure to be interested. Let us see! This page seems like solid matter as you look at it now. But, in reality, it is more like a cobweb than solid matter. The physicist knows it is composed of atoms. And how small is an atom? There are as many atoms in one drop of water as there are drops of water in the Mediterranean Sea, that there are as many atoms in one drop of water as there are blades of grass in all the world. And the atoms that make this paper are composed of what? Still smaller things called electrons and protons. These electrons are all rotating around the central proton of the atom, as far from it, relatively speaking, as the moon is from the earth. And they are swinging through their orbits, these electrons of this tiny universe, at the inconceivable speed of approximately ten thousand miles a second. So the electrons that compose this sheet of paper you are holding have moved since you began reading this very sentence, a distance equal to that which stretches between New York and Tokyo....

And only two minutes ago you may have thought this piece of paper was still and dull and dead; but, in reality, it is one of God's mysteries. It is a veritable cyclone of energy.

If you are interested in it now, it is because you have learned a new and strange fact about it. There lies one of the secrets of interesting people. That is a significant truth, one that we ought to profit by in our every day intercourse. The entirely new is not interesting; the entirely old has no attractiveness for us. We want to be told something new about the old. You cannot, for example, interest a farmer with a description of the Cathedral at Bourges, or the Mona Lisa. They are too new to him. There is no tie-up to his old interests. But you can interest him by relating the fact that farmers in Holland till land below the level of the sea and dig ditches to act as fences and build bridges to serve as gates. Your farmer will listen open-mouthed while you tell him that Dutch farmers keep the cows, during the winter, under the same roof that houses the family, and sometimes the cows look out through lace curtains at driving snows. He knows about cows and fences—new slants, you see, on old things. "Lace curtains! For a cow!" he'll exclaim. "I'll be jiggered!" And he will retail that story to his friends.

Here is a talk delivered by a student of this course. As you read it, see if it interests you. If it does, do you know why?

HOW SULPHURIC ACID AFFECTS YOU

Most liquids are measured by the pint, quart, gallon or barrel. We ordinarily speak of quarts of wine, gallons of milk, and barrels of molasses. When a new oil gusher is discovered, we speak of its output as so many barrels per day. There is one liquid, however, that is manufactured and consumed in such large quantities that the unit of measurement employed is the ton. This liquid is sulpheric acid.

It touches you in your daily life in a score of ways. If it were not for sulphuric acid, your car would stop, and you would go back to "old Dobbin" and the buggy, for it is used extensively in the refining of parafine and petrol. The electric lights that illuminate your office, that shine upon your dinner table, that show you the way to bed at night, would not be possible without it.

When you get up in the morning and turn on the water for your bath, you use a nickel-plated tap, which requires sulphuric acid in its manufacture. It was required also in the finishing of your enamelled tub. The soap you use has possibly been made from greases or oils that have been treated with the acid…. Your towel has made its acquaintance before you made the acquaintance of your towel. The bristles in your hairbrush have required it, and your celluloid comb could not have been produced without it. Your razor, no doubt, has been pickled in it after annealing.

You put on your underwear; you button up your outer garments. The bleacher, the manufacturer of dyes and the dyer himself used it. The button-maker possibly found the acid necessary to complete your buttons. The tanner used sulphuric acid in making the leather for your shoes, and it serves us again when we wish to polish them.

You come down to breakfast. The cup and saucer, if they be other than plain white, could not have come into being without it. It is used to produce the gilt and other ornamental colourings. Your spoon, knife and fork have seen a bath of sulphuric acid, if they be silver-plated.

The wheat of which your bread or rolls are made has possibly been grown by the use of a phosphate fertilizer, whose manufacture rests upon this acid.

And so on through the whole day, its work effects you at every turn. Go where you will, you cannot escape its influence. We can neither go to war without it nor live in peace without it. So it hardly seems possible that this acid, so essential to mankind, should be totally unfamiliar to the average man… But such is the case.

THE THREE MOST INTERESTING THINGS IN THE WORLD

What would you say they are—the three most interesting subjects in the world? Sex, property and religion. By the fist we can create life, by the second we maintain it, by the third we hope to continue it in the world to come.

But it is *our* sex, *our* property, *our* religion that interests us. Our interests swarm about our own egos.

We are not interested in a talk on How to Make Wills in Peru; but we may be interested in a talk entitled "How to Make Our Wills". We are not interested—except, perhaps, out of curiosity—in the religion of the Hindoo; but we are vitally interested in a religion that insures *us* unending happiness in the world to come.

When the late Lord Northcliffe was asked what interests people, he answered with one word—and that word was "themselves". Northcliffe ought to have known for he was the wealthiest newspaper owner in Great Britain.

Do you want to know what kind of person you are? Ah, now we are on an interesting topic. We are talking about *you*. Here is a way for *you* to hold the mirror up to your real self, and see *you* as *you* really are. Watch your reveries. What do we mean by reveries? Let Professor James Harvey Robinson answer. We are quoting from *The Mind in the Making*:

> We all appear to ourselves to be thinking all the time during our waking hours, and most of us are aware that we go on thinking while we are asleep, even more foolishly than when awake.

When uninterrupted by some practical issue we are engaged in what is known as a *reverie*. This is our spontaneous and favourite kind of thinking. We allow our ideas to take their own course and this course is determined by our hopes and fears, our spontaneous desires, their fulfilment or frustration, by our likes and dislikes, our loves and hates and resentments. *There is nothing else anything like so interesting to ourselves as ourselves.* All thought that is not more or less laboriously controlled and directed will inevitably circle about the beloved ego. It is amusing and pathetic to observe this tendency in ourselves and in others. We learn politely and generously to overlook this truth, but if we dare to think of it, it blazes forth like the noontide sun.

Our reveries from the chief index of our fundamental character. They are a reflection of our nature as modified by often hidden and forgotten experiences... The reverie doubtless influences all our speculations in its persistent tendency to self-magnification and self-justification, which are its chief preoccupations.

So remember that the people you are to talk to spend most of their time when they are not concerned with the problems of business, in thinking about and justifying and glorifying themselves. Remember that the average man will be more concerned about the cook leaving than about Italy paying her debts. He will be more wrought up over a dull razor blade than over a revolution in South America. His own toothache will distress him more than an earthquake in Asia destroying half a million lives. He would rather listen to you say some nice thing about him than hear you discuss the ten greatest men in history.

HOW TO BE A GOOD CONVERSATIONALIST

The reason so many people are poor conversationalists is because they talk about only the things that interests them. That may be deadly boring to others. Reverse the process. Lead the other person into talking about *his* interests, *his* business, *his* golf score, *his* success—or, if it is a mother, *her* children. Do that and listen intently and you will give pleasure;

consequently you will be considered a good conversationalist—even though you have done very little of the talking.

Mr. Harold Dwight recently made an extraordinarily successful speech at a banquet which marked the final session of a public speaking course. He talked about each man in turn around the entire table, told how he had talked when the course started, how he had improved; recalled the talks various members had made, the subjects they had discussed; he mimicked some of them, exaggerated their peculiarities, had everyone laughing, had everyone pleased. With such material, he could not possibly have failed. It was absolutely ideal. No other topic under the blue dome of Heaven would have so interested that group. Mr. Dwight knew how to handle human nature.

AN IDEA THAT ONE TWO MILLION READERS

A few years ago, the *American Magazine* enjoyed an amazing growth. Its sudden leap in circulation became one of the sensations of the publishing world. The secret? The secret was the late John M. Siddall and his ideas. When I first met Siddall he had charge of the Interesting People Department of that periodical. I had written a few articles for him; and one day he sat down and talked to me for a long time.

"People are selfish," he said. "They are interested chiefly in themselves. They are not very much concerned about whether the government should own the railroads; but they do want to know how to get ahead, how to draw more salary, how to keep healthy. If I were editor of this magazine," he went on,

> I would tell them how to take care of their teeth, how to take baths, how to keep cool in summer, how to get a position, how to handle employees, how to buy homes, how to remember, how to avoid grammatical errors, and so on. People are always interested in human stories, so I would have some rich man tell how he made a million. I would get prominent bankers and presidents of various corporations to tell the stories of how they battled their ways up from the ranks to power and wealth.

Shortly after that, Siddall was made editor. The magazine then had a small circulation, and was comparatively a failure. Siddall did just what he said he would do. The response? It was overwhelming. The circulation figures climbed up to two hundred thousand, three, four, half a million…. Here was something the public wanted. Soon a million people a month were buying it, then a million and a half, finally two millions. It did not stop there, but continued to grow for many years. Siddall appealed to the selfish interests of his readers.

HOW DR. CONWELL INTERESTED MILLIONS OF HEARERS

What was the secret of the world's most popular lecture, "Acres of Diamonds"? Just the thing we have been talking about. John M. Siddall discussed this lecture in the conversation I have just referred to, and I think its enormous success had something to do with determining the policy of his magazine.

It tells people how they can get ahead, how they can make more out of themselves in their present environment.

It was never a static lecture. Dr. Conwell made it personal to each town where he spoke. That was of immense importance. The local references made it appear fresh and new. They made that town, that audience, seem important. Here is his own story of how he did it:

> I visit a town or city, and try to arrive there early enough to see the postmaster, the barber, the keeper of the hotel, the principal of the schools, and the ministers of some of the churches, and then go into some of the factories and stores, and talk with the people, and get into sympathy with the local conditions of that town or city and see what has been their history, what opportunities they had, and what they had failed to do—and every town fails to do something—and then go to the lecture and talk to those people about the subjects which apply to their locality. Acres of Diamonds—the idea—has continuously been precisely the same. The idea is that in this country, every man has the opportunity to make more of himself than he does in his own environment, with his own skill, with his own energy, and with his own friends.

THE KIND OF SPEECH MATERIAL THAT
ALWAYS HOLDS ATTENTION

You may possibly bore people if you talk about things and ideas, but you can hardly fail to hold their attention when you talk about people. Tomorrow there will be millions of conversations floating over faces in the backyards, over tea tables and dinner tables—and what will be the predominating note in most of them? Personalities. He said this. Mrs. So-and-so did that. I saw her doing this, that and the other. He is making a fortune, and so on.

I have addressed many gatherings of schoolchildren, and I soon learned by experience that in order to keep them interested I had to tell them stories about people. As soon as I became general and dealt with abstract ideas, Johnny became restless and wriggled in his seat, Tommy made a face at someone, Billy threw something across the aisle.

True, these were audiences of children; but the intelligence tests used in the army during the last war revealed the startling fact that 49 per cent of the people in the United States have a mental age of about thirteen. So one can hardly go wrong in making a generous use of human interest stories. Our magazines that are read by millions are filled with them.

I once asked a group of businessmen in Paris to talk on How to Succeed. Most of them praised the homely virtues, preached at, lectured to, and bored their hearers. (Incidentally, I recently heard one of the most prominent businessmen make this identical mistake in a radio talk on this identical topic.)

So I halted this class, and said something like this:

We don't want to be lectured to. No one enjoys that. Remember you must be entertaining or we will pay no attention whatever to what you are saying. Also remember that one of the most interesting things in the world is sublimated, glorified gossip. So tell us the stories of two men you have known. Tell why one succeeded and why the other failed. We will gladly listen to that, remember it and possibly profit by it. It will also, by the way, be far easier for you to deliver than are these wordy, abstract preachments.

There was a certain member of that course who invariably found it difficult to interest either himself or his audience. This night, however, he seized the human story suggestion, and told us of two of his classmates in college. One of them had been so conservative that he had bought shirts at the different stores in town, and made charts showing which ones laundered best, wore longest and gave the most service for the money invested. His mind was always on pennies; yet, when he graduated—from an engineering college—he had such a high opinion of his own importance that he was not willing to begin at the bottom and work his way up, as the other graduates were doing. Even when the third annual reunion of the class came, he was still making laundry charts of his shirts, while waiting for some extraordinarily good thing to come his way. It never came. A quarter of a century has passed since then, and this man, dissatisfied and soured, still holds a minor position.

The speaker then contrasted with this failure the story of one of his classmates who had surpassed all expectations. This particular chap was a good mixer. Everyone liked him. Although he was ambitious to do big things later, he started as a draughtsman. But he was always on the lookout for opportunity. Plans were then being made for an exposition. He knew engineering talent would be needed there, so he resigned from his position and moved to the town of the exhibition. Through his agreeable personality, he soon won the friendship of a man with considerable influence. The two formed a partnership, and engaged immediately in the contracting business. They did considerable work for the telephone company, and this man was finally taken over by that concern at a large salary. Today he is a multimillionaire, one of the principal owners of Western Union.

We have recorded here only the bare outline of what the speaker told. He made his talk interesting and illuminating with a score of amusing and human details.... He talked on and on—this man who could not ordinarily find material for a three minute speech—and he was surprised beyond words to learn when he stopped that he had held the floor on this occasion for half an hour. The speech had been so interesting that it seemed short to everyone. It was this student's first real triumph.

Almost every student can profit by this incident. The average speech would be far more appealing if it were rich and replete with human interest stories. The speaker ought to attempt to make only a few points and to illustrate them with concrete cases. Such a method of speech building can hardly fail to get and hold attention.

If possible, these stories ought to tell of struggles, of things fought for an victories won. All of us are tremendously interested in fights and combats. There is an old saying that all the world loves a lover. It doesn't. What all the world loves is a scrap. It wants to see two lovers struggling for the hand of one woman. As an illustration of this fact, read almost any novel, magazine story, or go to see almost any film drama. When all the obstacles are removed and the reputed hero takes the so-called heroin in his arms, the audience begins reaching for their hats and coats. Five minutes later the sweeping women are gossiping over their broom handles.

Almost all magazine fiction is based on this formula. Make the reader like the hero or heroine. Make him or her long for something intensely. Make that something seem impossible to get. Show how the hero or heroine fights and gets it.

The story of how a man battled in business or profession against discouraging odds and won is always inspiring, always interesting. A magazine editor once told me that the real, inside story of any person's life is entertaining. If one has struggled and fought—and who hasn't—his story, if correctly told, will appeal. There can be no doubt of that.

BE CONCRETE

The writer once had in the same course in public speaking, a Doctor of Philosophy and rough-and-ready fellow who had spent his youth thirty years ago in the British Navy. The Polished Scholar was a university professor; his classmate from the seven seas was the proprietor of a small side street moving-van establishment. Strange to say, the moving-van man's talks during the course would have held a popular audience far better than the talks of the college professor. Why? The college man spoke in beautiful English, with a demeanour of culture and refinement, and with logic and clearness; but his talks lacked one essential, *concreteness*. They were too vague, too general. On the other hand, the van owner possessed hardly enough power of celebration to generalize. When he talked he got right down to business immediately. He was definite; he was concrete. That quality, coupled with his virility and his fresh phraseology, made his talks very entertaining.

I have cited this instance, not because it is typical either of college men or moving-van proprietors, but because it illustrates the interest-getting power that accrues to the man—regardless of education—who has the happy habit of being concrete and definite in his speaking.

This principle is so important that we are going to use several illustrations to try to lodge it firmly in your mind. We hope you will never forget it, never neglect it.

Is it, for example, more interesting to state that Martin Luther, as a boy, was "stubborn and intractable", or is it better to say that he confessed that his teachers had flogged him as often as "fifteen times in a forenoon"?

Words like "stubborn and intractable" have very little attention value. But isn't it easy to listen to the flogging count?

The old method of writing a biography was to deal in a lot of generalities which Aristotle called, and rightly called, "The refuge of weak minds." The new method is to deal with concrete facts that speak for themselves. The old-fashioned biographer said that John Doe was born of "poor but honest parents". The new method would say that John Doe's father couldn't afford a pair of overshoes, so when the snow came, he had to tie gunny sacking around his shoes to keep his feet dry and warm; but, in spite of his poverty, he never watered the milk and he never traded a horse with the heaves as a sound animal. That shows that his parents were "poor but honest", doesn't it? And doesn't it do it in a way that is far more interesting than the "poor but honest" method?

If this method works for modern biographers it will work also for modern speakers.

Let us take one more illustration. Suppose you wished to state that the potential horse power wasted at Niagara every day was appalling. Suppose you said just that, and then added, that if it were utilized and the resulting profits turned to purchasing the necessities of life, crowds could be clothed and fed. Would that be the way to make it interesting and entertaining? No—No. Isn't this far better? We are quoting from Edwin E. Slosson in the *Daily Science News Bulletin*:

We are told that there are some millions of people in poverty and poorly nourished in this country, yet here at Niagara is wasted the equivalent of 250,000 loaves of bread an hour. We may see with our mind's eye 600,000 nice fresh eggs dropping over the precipice every hour and making a gigantic omelette in the whirlpool. If calico were continuously pouring from the looms in a stream 4,000 feet wide like Niagara River, it would represent the same destruction of property. If a Carnegie Library were held under the spout it would be filled with good books in an hour or two. Or we can imagine a big department store floating down from Lake Erie every day and smashing its varied contents on the rocks 160 feet below. That would be an exceedingly interesting and diverting spectacle, quite as attractive to the crowd as the present, and no more expensive to maintain. Yet some people might object to that on the ground of extravagance who now object to the utilization of the power of the falling water.

PICTURE-BUILDING WORDS

In this process of interest-getting, there is one aid, one technique, that is of the highest importance; yet it is all but ignored. The average speaker does not seem to be aware of its existence. He has probably never consciously thought about it at all. I refer to the process of using words that create pictures. The speaker who is easy to listen to is the one who sets images floating before your eyes. The one who employs foggy, commonplace, colourless symbols sets the audience to nodding.

Pictures. Pictures. Pictures. They are as free as the air you breathe. Sprinkle them through your talks, your conversation, and you will be more entertaining, more influential.

To illustrate, let us take the excerpt just quoted from the *Daily Science News Bulletin* regarding Niagara. Look at the picture words. They leap up and go scampering away in every sentence, as thick as rabbits in Australia: "250,000 loaves of bread, 600,000 eggs dropping over the precipice, gigantic omelette in the whirlpool, calico pouring from the looms in a stream 4,000 feet wide, Carnegie library held under the spout, books, a big department store floating, smashing, rocks below, falling water."

It would be almost as difficult to ignore such a talk or article as it would be to pay not the slightest attention to the scenes from a film unwinding on the silver screen of the motion picture theatre.

Picture-building phrases swarm through the pages of the Bible and through Shakespeare like bees around a cider mill. For example, a commonplace writer would have said that a certain thing would be super-fluous, like trying to improve the perfect. How did Shakespeare express the same thought? With a picture phrase that is immortal" "To gild refined gold, to paint the lily, to throw perfume on the violet."

Did you ever pause to observe that the proverbs that are passed on from generation to generation are almost all visual sayings?" A bird in the hand is worth two in the bush." "It never rains but it pours." "You can lead a horse to water but you can't make him drink." And you will find the same picture element in almost all the similes that have lived for centuries and grown hoary with too much use: "Sly as a fox." "Dead as a door nail." "Flat as a pancake." "Hard as a rock."

Lincoln continually talked in visual terminology. When he became annoyed with the long, complicated, red-tape reports that came to his desk in the White House, he objected to them, not with a colourless phrase-ology, but with a picture phrase that it is almost impossible to forget. "When I send a man to buy a horse," said he, "I don't want to be told how many hairs the horse has in his tail. I wish only to know his points."

THE INTEREST-GETTING VALUE OF CONTRASTS

Listen to the following condemnation of Charles I by Macaulay.

Note that Macaulay not only uses pictures, but he also employs balanced sentences. Violent contrasts almost always hold our interests; violent contrasts are the very brick and mortar of this paragraph:

> We charge him with having broken his coronation oath; and we are told that he kept his marriage vow! We accuse him of having given up his people to the merciless inflictions of the most hot-headed of

prelates; and the defence is that he took his little son on his knee and kissed him! We censure him for having violated the articles of the Petition of Right, after having, for good and valuable consideration, promised to observe them; and we are informed that he was accustomed to hear prayers at six o'clock in the morning! It is to such considerations as these, together with his Vandyke dress, his handsome face and his peaked beard, that he owes, we verily believe, most of his popularity with the present generation.

INTEREST IS CONTAGIOUS

We have been discussing so far the kind of material that interests and audience. However, one might mechanically follow all the suggestions made here and speak according to Cocker, and yet be vapid and dull. Catching and holding the interest of people is a delicate thing, a matter of feeling and spirit. It is not like operating a steam engine. No book of precise rules can be given for it.

Interest, be it remembered, is contagious. Your hearers are almost sure to catch it if you have a bad case of it yourself. A short time ago, a gentleman rose during a session of this course and warned his audience that if the present methods of catching rock fish were continued, the species would become extinct. And in a very few years! He felt his subject. It was important. He was in real earnest about it. Everything about his matter and manner showed that. When he arose to speak, I did not know that there was such an animal as a rock fish. I imagine that most of the audience shared my lack of knowledge and lack of interest. But before the speaker finished, all of us had caught something of his concern. All of us would probably have been willing to have signed a petition to the legislature to protect the rock fish by law.

I once asked Richard Washburn Child, then American Ambassador to Italy, the secret of his success as an interesting writer. He replied: "I am so excited about life that I cannot keep still. I just have to tell people about it." One cannot keep from being enthralled with a speaker or writer like that.

I recently went to hear a speaker in London: after he was through, one of our party, the late E.F. Benson, a well-known English novelist, remarked that he enjoyed the last part of the talk far more than the first. When I asked him why, he replied: "The speaker himself seemed more interested in the last part, and I always rely on the speaker to supply the enthusiasm and interest."

Everyone does. Remember that.

> *"Always have something to say. The man who has something to say, and who is known never to speak unless he has, is sure to be listened to."*
>
> **—Lord Bryce**

> *"There is in all communication—written or spoken—a certain dead line of interest. If we can cross that dead line, we have the world with us—temporarily at least. If we cannot cross it, we may as well retire. The world will have none of us."*
>
> **—H.A. Overstreet**

> *"My ultimate aim would be to captivate an audience, even just for a second."*
>
> **—Tabrett Bethell**

CHAPTER 13

···

Capturing Your Audience at Once

*"A good teacher, like a good entertainer, first must hold his
audience's attention, then he can teach his lesson."*

—John Henrik Clarke

Several years ago a fuel and iron company was suffering from labour troubles. Shooting had taken place; there had been bloodshed. The air was electric with bitter hatreds. The very name of Rockefeller was anathema. Yet John D. Rockefeller Jr. wanted to talk to the employees of that concern. He wanted to explain, to persuade them to his way of thinking, to get them to accept his beliefs. He realized that in the very opening of his speech he must eradicate all ill-feeling. All antagonism. At the very outset, he did it beautifully and sincerely. Most public speakers can study his method with profit:

> This is a red-letter day in my life. It is the first time I have ever had the good fortune to meet the representatives of the employees of this great company, its officers and superintendents, together, and I can assure you that I am proud to be here, and that I shall remember this gathering for as long as I live. Had this meeting been held two weeks ago, I should have stood here a stranger to most of you, recognizing few faces. Having had the opportunity last week of visiting all the camps in the southern coalfields and of talking individually with practically all of the representatives, except those who were away; having visited in your homes, met

many of your wives and children, we meet here not as strangers but as friends, and it is in this spirit of mutual friendship that I am glad to have this opportunity to discuss with you our common interests.

Since this is a meeting of the officers of the company and the representatives of the employees, it is only by your courtesy that I am here, for I am not so fortunate as to be either one or the other; and yet I feel that I am intimately associated with you men, for, in a sense, I represent both the stockholders and the directors.

This is tact—supreme tact. And the speech, in spite of the bitter hatred that had existed, was successful. The men who had been striking and fighting for higher wages never said anything more about it after Rockefeller had explained all the facts in the situation.

A DROP OF HONEY AND TWO-GUN MEN

"It is an old and true maxim 'That a drop of honey catches more flies than a gallon of gall.' So with men. If you would win a man to your cause, first convince him that you are his sincere friend. Therein is a drop of honey that catches his heart; which, say what he will, is the great high road to his reason, and when once gained, you will find but little trouble in convincing his judgment of the justice of your cause. If indeed that cause really be a just one."

That was Lincoln's plan. In 1858, during his campaign for the United States Senate, he was announced to speak in what was, at that time, the semi-barbarous part of Southern Illinois called "Egypt". They were a rough lot, the men in that section, and they carried ugly-looking knives and pistols strapped to their belts even on public occasions. Their hatred of all antislavery men was equalled only by their love of fighting and whiskey made from Indian corn. Southern men, some of them slave owners from Kentucky and Missouri, had crossed over the Mississippi and the Ohio to be on hand for the excitement and trouble. Plenty of it was in prospect, for the rougher elements had sworn that, if Lincoln tried to talk, they would "run the damned Abolitionist out of town", and "shoot him to fiddle strings".

Lincoln had heard these threats, and he knew the intense feeling that existed, the positive danger. "But if only they will give me a fair chance to say a few opening words," he declared, "I'll fix them all right". So, before beginning to talk, he had himself introduced to the ringleaders, and shook their hands cordially. He made one of the most tactful openings I have ever read:

Fellow citizens of Southern Illinois, fellow citizens of the State of Kentucky, fellow citizens of Missouri—I am told there are some of you here present who would like to make trouble for me. I don't understand why they should. I am a plain, common man, like the rest of you; and why should I not have as good a right to speak my sentiments as the rest of you? Why, good friends, I am one of you. I am not an interloper here. I was born in Kentucky, and raised in Illinois, just like the most of you, and worked my way along by hard scratching. I know the people of Kentucky, and I know the people of Southern Illinois, and I think I know the Missourains. I am one of them, and therefore ought to know them; and they ought to know me better, and, if they did know me better, they would know that I am disposed to make them trouble. Then, why should they, or any one of them, want to make trouble for me? Don't do any such foolish thing, fellow citizens. Let us be friends, and treat each other like friends. I am one of the humblest and most peaceful men in the world—would wrong no man, would interfere with no man's rights. And all I ask is that, having something to say, you give me decent hearing. And, being Illinoisans, Kentuckians, and Missourians—brave and gallant people—I feel sure that you will do that. And now let us reason together, like the honest fellows we are.

As he spoke these words, his face was the very picture of good nature, and his voice vibrated with sympathetic earnestness. That tactful opening calmed the oncoming storm, silenced his enemies. In fact, it transformed many of them into friends. They cheered his speech and, later, those rough and rude "Egyptians" were among his most ardent supporters for the Presidency.

"Interesting," you remark, "but what has all this got to do with me? I am no Rockefeller; I am not going to address hungry strikers longing to strangle and batter the life out of me. I am no Lincoln; I am not going to talk to two-gun desperadoes full of corn whiskey and hatred."

True, true, but aren't you, almost every day of your life, talking to people who differ from you on some subject under discussion? Aren't you constantly trying to win people to your way of thinking—at home, in the office, in the market place? Is there room for improvement in your methods? How do you begin? By showing Lincoln's tact? And Rockefeller's? If so, you are a person of rare finesse and extraordinary discretion. Most men begin, not by thinking about the other fellow's views and desires, not by trying to find a common ground of agreement, but by unloading their own opinions.

For example, I have heard hundreds of speeches on the hotly contested subject of prohibition. In almost every instance, the speaker, with all the tact of a bull in a china shop, opened with some positive and perhaps belligerent statement. He showed once and for all which direction he faced and under which flag he fought. He showed that his mind was made up so firmly that there was not the slightest chance of it being changed; yet he was expecting others to abandon their cherished beliefs and to accept his. The effect? About the same that results from all arguments: no one was convinced. Instantly, he lost by his blunt, aggressive opening the sympathetic attention of all who differed with him; instantly, they discounted all he said and would say; instantly, they challenged his statements; instantly, they held his opinions in contempt. His talk served but to entrench them more strongly behind the bulwark of their own beliefs.

You see, he made, at the very outset, the fatal mistake of prodding his listeners, of getting them bending backwards and saying through their shut teeth: "No! No! No!"

Is not that a very serious situation if one wishes to win converts to his way of thinking? A most illuminating statement on this point is the following quotation from Professor Overstreet's lectures before the school for Social Research.

"A 'No' response is a most difficult handicap to overcome. When a person has said 'No', all his pride of personality demands that he remain consistent with himself. He may later feel that the 'No' was ill advised; nevertheless, there is his precious pride to consider! Once having said a thing, he must stick to it. Hence it is of the very greatest importance that we start a person in the affirmative direction...." The skillful speaker gets

at the outset a number of "yes-responses". He has thereby set the psychological processes of his listeners moving in the affirmative direction. It is like the movement of a billiard ball. Propel it in one direction, send it takes some force to deflect it; far more force to and it back in the opposite direction.

The psychological patterns here are quite clear. When a person says "No" and really means it, he is doing far more than saying a word of two letters. His entire organism—glandular, nervous, muscular—gathers itself together into a condition of rejection. There is, usually in minute but sometimes in observable degree, a physical withdrawal, or readiness for withdrawal. The whole neuro-muscular system, in short, sets itself on guard against acceptance. Where, on the contrary, a person says "Yes", none of the withdrawing activities take place. The organism is in a forward-moving, accepting, open attitude. Hence the more "Yeses" we can, at the very outset, induce, the more likely we are to succeed in capturing the attention for our ultimate proposal.

It is a very simple technique—this yes-response. And yet how much neglected! It often seems as if people get a sense of their own importance by antagonizing at the outset. The radical comes into a conference with his conservative brethren; and immediately he must make them furious! What, as a matter of fact, is the good of it? If he simply does it in order to get some pleasure out of it for himself, he may be pardoned. But if he expects to achieve something, he is only psychologically stupid.

Get a student to say "No" at the beginning, or a customer, child, husband, or wife, and it takes the wisdom and the patience of angels to transform that bristling negative into an affirmative.

How is one going to get these desirable "yes-responses" at the very outset? Fairly simple. "My way of opening and winning an argument," confided Lincoln, "is to first find a common ground of agreement." Lincoln found it even when he was discussing the highly inflammable subject of slavery. "For the first half –hour," declared *The Mirror,* a neutral paper reporting one of his talks, "his opponents would agree with every word he uttered. From that point he began to lead them off, little by little, until it seemed as if he had got them all into his fold."

SENATOR LODGE'S WAY OF DOING IT

Shortly after the close of World War I, the late Senator Lodge and President Lowell of Harvard were scheduled to debate the League of Nations question before a Boston audience. Senator Lodge felt that most of the audience were hostile to his view; yet he must win them to his way of thinking. How? By a direct, frontal, aggressive attack on their convictions? Ah, no. The Senator was far too shrewd a psychologist to bugle his plea with such crude tactics. He began with supreme tact, with admirable finesse. The opening of his speech is quoted in the following paragraph. Note that even his most bitter opponents could not have differed with the sentiments expressed in his first dozen sentences. Note how he appeals to their emotion of patriotism in his salutation: "My Fellow Americans." Observe how he minimizes the differences in the views they are to defend, and how he deftly stresses the things they cherish in common.

See how he praises his opponent, how he insists upon the fact that they differ only on minor details of method, and not at all upon the vital question of the welfare of America and the peace of the world. He even goes further and admits that he is in favour of a League of Nations of some kind. So, in the last analysis, he differed from his opponent only in this: he felt that we ought to have a more ideal and efficacious League.

Your Excellency, Ladies and Gentlemen, My Fellow Americans:

I am largely indebted to President Lowell for this opportunity to address this great audience. He and I are friends of many years, both Republicans. He is the president of our great university, one of the most important and influential places in the United States. He is also an eminent student and historian of politics and government. He and I may differ as to methods in this great question now before the people, but I am sure that in regard to the security of the peace of the world and the welfare of the United States we do not differ in purposes.

"I am going to say a single word, if you will permit me, as to my own position. I have tried to state it over and over again. I thought I had stated it in plain English. But there are those who find in misrepresentation a convenient weapon for controversy, and there are others, most excellent people, who perhaps have not seen what I have said and who possibly have misunderstood me. It has been said that I am against any League of Nation. I am not; far from it. I am anxious to have the nations, the free nations of the world, united in a league, as we call it, a society, as the French call it., but united peace of the world and to bring about a general disarmament.

No matter how determined you were beforehand to differ with a speaker, an opening like that would make you soften and relent a bit, wouldn't it? Wouldn't it make you willing to listen to more? Wouldn't it tend to convince you of the speaker's fair mindedness?

What would have been the result had Senator Lodge set out immediately to show those who believed in the League of Nations that they were hopelessly in error, cherishing a delusion? The result would have been futile; the following quotation from Professor James Harvey Robinson's enlightening and popular book *The Mind in the Making* shows the psychological reason why such an attack would have been futile:

We sometimes find ourselves changing our minds without any resistance of heavy emotion, but if we are told we are wrong we resent the imputation and harden our hearts. We are incredibly heedless in the formation of our beliefs, but find ourselves filled with an illicit passion for them when anyone proposes to rob us of their companionship. It is obviously not the ideas themselves that are dear to us, but our self-esteem which is threatened.... The little word *my* is the most important one in human affairs, and properly to reckon with it is the beginning of wisdom. It has the same force whether it is *my* dinner, *my* dog and *my* house, or *my* faith, *my* country and *my* God. We not only resent the imputation that our watch is wrong, or our car shabby, but that our conception of the canals of Mars, of the pronunciation of 'Epictetus', of the medicinal value of salicine, or of the date of Sargon I, are subject to revision.... We like to continue to believe what we have been accustomed to accept as true, and the resentment aroused when doubt is cast upon any of our assumptions leads us to seek every manner of excuse for clinging to it. The result is that most of our so-called reasoning consists in finding arguments for going on believing as we already do.

THE BEST ARGUMENT IS AN EXPLANATION

Is it not quite evident that the speaker who argues with his audience is merely arousing their stubbornness, putting them on the defensive, making it well nigh impossible for them to change their minds? Is it wise to start by saying, "I am going to prove so and so?" Aren't your hearers liable to accept that as a challenge and remark silently, "Let's see you do it."

Is it not much more advantageous to begin by stressing something that you and all of your hearers believe, and then to raise some pertinent question that everyone would like to have answered? Then take your audience with you in an earnest for the answer. While on that search, present the facts as you see them so clearly that they will unconsciously be led to accept your conclusions as their own. They will have much more faith is some truth that they believe they have discovered for themselves. "The best argument is that which seems merely an explanation."

In every controversy, no matter how wide and bitter the differences, there is always some common ground of agreement on which the speaker can invite everyone to assemble for the search after facts that he is going to conduct. To illustrate: even if the head of the Communist Party were addressing a convention of the Banker's Association, he could find some mutual beliefs, some analogous desires to share with his hearers. Couldn't he? Let us see:

Poverty has always been one of the cruel problems of human society. We have always felt it our duty to alleviate, whenever and wherever possible, the sufferings of the poor. We are a generous nation. No other people in all history have poured out their wealth so prodigally, so unselfishly to help the unfortunate. Now, with this same mental generosity and spiritual unselfishness that has characterized our givings in the past, let us examine together the facts of our industrial life and see if we can find some means, fair and just and acceptable to all, that will tend to prevent as well as to mitigate the evils of poverty.

Who could object to that? Could Father Coughlin, or Norman Thomas, or J. Pierpont Morgan? Hardly.

Do we seem to be contradicting here the gospel of force and energy and enthusiasm? Hardly. There is a time for everything. But the time for force is seldom in the beginning of a talk. Tact is more likely to be needed then.

HOW PATRICK HENRY LAUNCHED HIS STORMY ADDRESS

Every schoolboy in the land is familiar with the fiery close of Patrick Henry's famous speech before the Virginia Convention of 1775: "Give me liberty or give me death." But few of them realize the comparative calm, the tactful manner in which Henry launched that stormy and emotional and history-making address. Should the American colonies separate from and go to war with England? The question was being debated with intense passion. Feelings flamed at white heat, yet Patrick Henry began by complimenting the abilities and praising the patriotism of those who opposed him. Note, in the second paragraph, how he gets his audience thinking with him by asking questions, by letting them draw their own conclusions:

> Mr. President: No man thinks more highly than I do of the patri-
> otism, as well as abilities, of the very worthy gentlemen who have
> just addressed the house. But different men often see the same
> subject in different lights; and, therefore, I hope it will not be
> thought disrespectful to those gentlemen, if, entertaining as I do
> opinions of a character very opposite to theirs, I shall speak forth my
> sentiments freely, and without reserve. This is no time for ceremony.

The question before the house is one of awful moment to the country. For my own part, I consider it as nothing less than a question of freedom or slavery. And in proportion to the magnitude of the subject ought to be the freedom of the debate. It is only in this way that we can hope to arrive at truth, and fulfill the great responsibility which we hold to God and our country. Should I keep back my opinions at such a time, through fear of giving offence, I should consider myself as guilty of treason towards my country, and of an act of disloyalty toward the Majesty of Heaven, which I revere above all earthly things.

Mr. President, it is natural to man to indulge in the illusions of hope. We are apt to shut our eyes again a painful truth, and listen to the song of that Siren till she transforms us into beasts. Is this the part of wise men, engaged in a great and arduous struggle of liberty? Are we disposed to be of the number of those who, having eyes see not, having ears hear not, the things which so nearly concern their temporal salvation? For my part, whatever anguish of spirit it may cost, I am willing to know the whole truth; to know the worst and to provide for it.

THE BEST SPEECH SHAKESPEARE WROTE

The most famous speech that Shakespeare put into the mouth of any of his characters—Mark Antony's funeral oration over the body of Julius Caesar—is a classic example of supreme tact.

This was the situation. Caesar had become dictator. Naturally, inevitably, a score of his political enemies were envious, and were eager to tear him down, to destroy him, to make his power their own. Twenty-three of them banded together under the leadership of Brutus and Cassius and thrust their daggers into his body…. Mark Antony had been Caesar's Secretary of State. He was a handsome chap, this Antony, a ready writer, a powerful speaker. He could represent the government well at public affairs. Small wonder Caesar had chosen him as his right hand man. Now, with Caesar out of the way, what should the conspirators do with Antony? Remove him? Kill him? There had been enough bloodshed already; there was enough to justify as it was. Why not win this Antony to their side, why not use his undeniable influence, his moving eloquence, to shield them and further their own ends? Sounded safe and reasonable, so they tried it. They saw him and went so far as to permit him to "say a few words" over the corpse of the man who had all but ruled the world....

Antony mounts the rostrum in the Roman Forum. Before him lies the murdered Caesar. A mob surges noisily and threateningly about Antony, a rabble friendly to Brutus, Cassius and the other assassins. Antony's purpose is to turn this popular enthusiasm into intense hatred, to stir the plebeians to rise in mutiny and slay those that had struck Caesar down. He raises his hands, the tumult ceases, he starts to speak. Note how ingeniously, how adroitly he begins, praising Brutus and the other conspirators:

> For Brutus is an honorable man;
> So are they all, all honorable men.

Observe that he does not argue. Gradually, unobtrusively, he presents certain facts about Caesar; tells how the ransom from his captives filled the general coffers, how he wept when the poor cried, how he refused a crown, how he willed his estates to the public. He presents the facts, asks the mob questions, and lets them draw their own conclusions. The evidence is presented, not as something new, but as something they had for the moment forgotten:

I tell you that which you yourselves do know.

And with a magic tongue through it all, he whipped up their feelings, stirred their emotions, aroused their pity, heated their anger. Antony's Masterpiece of tact and eloquence is given here in its entirety. Search where you will, range through all the broad fields of literature and oratory, and I doubt if you will find half a dozen speeches to equal this. It merits the serious study of every man who aspires to excel in the fine art of influencing human nature. But there is another reason, entirely aside from the one we are considering now, why Shakespeare ought to be read and reread by businessmen; he possessed a larger vocabulary than did any other writer who ever lived; he used words more magically, more beautifully. No one can study *Macbeth* and *Hamlet* and *Julius Caesar* without unconsciously brightening and widening and refining his own diction.

Ant. Friends, Romans, countrymen, lend me your ears:

I come to bury Caesar, not to praise him.

The evil that men do lives after them;

The good is oft interred with their bones:

So let it be with Caesar. The noble Brutus Hath told you Caesar was ambitious:

If it were so, It was a grievous fault;

And grievously hath Caesar answer'd it.

Here, under leave of Brutus and the rest—

For Brutus is an honourable man;

So are they all, all honourable men—

Come I to speak in Caesar's funeral.

He was my friend, faithful and just to me:

But Brutus says he was ambitious;

And Brutus is an honourable man.

Ha hath brought many captives home to Rome,

Whose ransoms did the general coffers fill:

Did this in Caesar seem ambitious?

When that the poor have cried, Caesar hath wept:

Ambition should be made of sterner stuff:

Yet Brutus says he was ambitious;

And Brutus is an honourable man.

You all did see that on the Lupercal I thrice presented him a kingly crown,

Which he did thrice refuse. Was this ambition?

Yet Brutus says he was ambitious;

And, sure, he is an honourable man.

Speak not to disprove what Brutus spoke.

But here I am, to speak what I do know.

You all did love him once—not without cause;

What cause withholds you, then, to mourn for him?

O judgment, thou fled to brutish beasts,

And men have lost their reason! Bear with me;
My heart is in the coffin there with Caesar,
And I must pause till it come back to me.
Cit. Methinks there is much reason in his sayings.
Cit. If thou consider rightly of the matter,
Caesar has had great wrong.
Cit. Has he not, masters?
I fear there will a worse come in his place.
Cit. Mark'd ye his words? He would not take the crown
Therefore 'tis certain he was not ambitious.
Cit. If it be found so, some will dear abide it.
Cit. Poor soul! his eyes are red as fire with weeping.
Cit. There's not a nobler man in Rome than Antony.
Cit. Now mark him; he begins again to speak.
Ant. But yesterday the word of Caesar might
Have stood against the world: now lies he there,
And none so poor to do him reverence.
O masters, if I were dispos'd to stir
Your hearts and minds to mutiny and rage,
I should do Brutus wrong, and Cassius wrong,
Who, you all know, are honourable men.
I will not do them wrong: I rather choose
To wrong the
dead, to wrong myself, and you,
Then I will wrong such honourable men.
But here's parchment with the seal of Caesar,—
I found it in his closet,—'tis his will:
Let but the commons hear this testament (Which, pardon me,
I do not mean to read),
And they would go and kiss dead Caesar's wounds,
And dip their napkins in his sacred blood;
Yea, beg a hair of him for memory,

And, dying, mention it within their wills,

Bequeathing it as a rich legacy Unto their issue.

4 Cit. We'll hear the will; read it, Mark Antony.

Citizens. The will, the will! We will hear Caesar's will.

Ant. Have patience, gentle friends; I must not read it:

It is not meet you know how Caesar lov'd you.

You are not wood, you are not stones, but men;

And, being men, hearing the will of Caesar,

It will inflame you, it will make you mad.

'Tis good you know not that you are his heirs;

For, if you should, O what would come of it!

4 Cit. Read the will! we'll hear it, Antony;

You shall read us the will—Caesar's will!

Ant. Will you be patient? Will you stay awhile?

I have o'ershot myself, to tell you of it.

I fear I wrong the honourable men

Whose daggers have stabb'd Caesar; I do fear it.

4 Cit. They were traitors: honourable men!

Citizens. The will! The testament!

4 Cit. They were villains, murderers. The will!

Read the will!

Ant. You will compel me, then, to read the will?

Then make a ring about the corpse of Caesar,

And let me show you him that made the will.

Shall I descend? and will you give me leave?

Citizens. Come down.

2. Cit. Descend. [*He comes down*]

3. Cit. You shall have leave.

4. Cit. A ring! stand round.

1. Cit. Stand from hearse; stand from the body.

2. Cit. Room for Antony!—most noble Antony!

Ant. Nay, press not so upon me; stand far off.

Citizens. Stand back; room! bear back.

Ant. If you have tears, prepare to shed them now.

You all do know this mantle: I remember

The first time ever Caesar put it on;

'Twas on a summer's evening, in his tent,

That day he overcame the Nervii.

Look, in this place ran Cassius' dagger through:

See what a rent the envious Casca made:

Through this the well-beloved Brutus stabb'd;

And, as he pluck'd his cursed steel away,

Mark how the blood of Caesar follow'd it,—

As rushing out of doors, to be resolv'd If Brtutus so unkindly knock'd,

or no;

For Brutus, as you know, was Caesar's angel:

Judge, O you gods, how dearly Caesar lov'd him!

This was the most unkindest cut of all;

For, when the noble Caesar saw him stab,

Ingratitude, more strong than traitor's arms,

Quite vanquish'd him: then burst his mighty heart;

And, in his mantle muffling up his face,

Even at the base of Pompey's statue,

Which all the while ran blood, great Caesar fell.

O, what a fall was there, my countrymen!

Then I, and you, and all of us fell down,

Whilst bloody treason flourish'd over us.

O, now you weep; and, I perceive, you feel

The dint of pity: these are gracious drops.

Kind souls, what, weep you, when you but behold

Our Caesar's vesture wounded? Look you here,

Here is himself, marr'd, as you see, with traitors.

1 Cit. O piteous spectacle!

2. Cit. O noble Caesar!

3. *Cit.* O woeful day!

4. *Cit.* O traitors, villains!

1. *Cit.* O most bloody sight!

2. *Cit.* We will be reveng'd.

Citizens. Revenge—about—seek—burn—fire—kill slay—let not a traitor live!

Ant. Stay, countrymen.

1. *Cit.* Peace there! Hear the noble Antony.

2. *Cit.* We'll hear him, we'll follow him, we'll die with him.

Ant. Good friends, sweet friends, let me not stir you up
To such a sudden flood of mutiny.
They that have done this deed are honourable:
What private griefs they have, alas, I know not,
That made them don't; they're wise and honourable,
And will, no doubt, with reasons answer you.
I come not, friends, to steal away your hearts:
I am no orator, as Brutus is;
But, as you know me all, a plain blunt man,
That love my friend; and that they know full well
That gave me public leave to speak of him.
For I have neither wit, nor words, nor worth,
Action, nor utterance, nor the power of speech,
To stir men's blood: I only speak right on;
I tell you that which you yourselves do know;
Show you sweet Caesar's wounds, poor, poor dumb mouths,
And bid them speak for me: but were I Brutus,
And Brutus Antony, there were an Antony
Would ruffle up your spirit, and put a tongue
In every wound of Caesar, that should move
The stones of Rome to rise and mutiny.
Citizens. We'll mutiny.

1. *Cit.* We'll burn the house of Brutus.

3. *Cit.* Away, then! come, seek the conspirators.

Ant. Yet hear me, countrymen; yet hear me speak.

Citizens. Peace, ho! Hear Antony; most noble Antony.

Ant. Why, friends, you go to do you know not what.

Wherein hath Caesar thus deserv'd your loves?

Alas, you know not; I must tell you, then:

You have forgot the will I told you of.

Citizens. Most true; the will!—let's stay, and hear the will.

Ant. Here is the will, and under Caesar's seal.

To every Roman citizen he gives.

To every several man, seventy-five drachmas.

2. *Cit.* Most noble Caesar!—we'll revenge his death.

3. *Cit.* O, royal Caesar!

Ant. Hear me with patience.

Citizens. Peace, ho!

Ant. Moreover, he hath left you all his walks,

His private arbours, and new-planted orchards,

On this side Tiber; he hath left them to you,

And to your heirs for ever; common pleasures,

To walk abroad, and recreate yourselves.

Here was a Caesar! When comes such another?

1 *Cit.* Never, never.—Come, away, away!

We'll burn his body in the holy place,

And with the brands fire the traitors' houses.

Take up the body.

2. *Cit.* Go, fetch fire.

3. *Cit.* Pluck down benches.

4. *Cit.* Pluck down forms, windows, anything.

[*Exeunt Citizens with the body. Ant.* Now let it work:—

Mischief, thou art afoot,

Take thou what course thou wilt!]

"You have to respect your audience. Without them, you're essentially standing alone, singing to yourself."

—K.D. Lang

"If the audience knew what they wanted then they wouldn't be the audience, they would be the artist."

—Alan Moore

OTHER HARDBACK BOOKS

- 1984 by George Orwell
  Fiction/Classics, ISBN: 9788193545836

- Abraham Lincoln by Lord Charnwood
  Biographies/Leaders, ISBN: 9789387669147

- Alice's Adventures in Wonderland by Lewis Carroll
  Children's/Classics, ISBN: 9789387669055

- Animal Farm by George Orwell
  Fiction/Classics, ISBN: 9789387669062

- Anthem by Ayn Rand
  Fiction/Classics, ISBN: 9789389157178

- As a Man Thinketh by James Allen
  Fiction/Classics, ISBN: 9789388118422

- Awakened Imagination by Neville Goddard
  Religion & Spirituality, ISBN: 9789389157185

- Be What You Wish by Neville Goddard
  Mind, Body & Spirit, ISBN: 9789388118163

- Becoming a Writer by Dorothea Brande
  Self Help/General, ISBN: 9789389157192

- Believe in Yourself by Joseph Murphy
  Mind, Body & Spirit, ISBN: 9789388118439

- Black Beauty by Anna Sewell
  Children's/Classics, ISBN: 9789388118262

- Civilization and Its Discontents by Sigmund Freud
  Social Sciences/General, ISBN: 9789388118279

- Demian by Hermann Hesse
  Fiction/Classics, ISBN: 9789388118170

- Feeling is the Secret by Neville Goddard
  Religion & Spirituality, ISBN: 9789389157208

OTHER HARDBACK BOOKS

- Gitanjali by Rabindranath Tagore
  Fiction/Poems, ISBN: 9789387669079

- Great Speeches of Abraham Lincoln by Abraham Lincoln
  History/United States, ISBN: 9789387669154

- How to Attract Money by Joseph Murphy
  Self Help/Success, ISBN: 9789388118446

- How to be Filled with the Holy Spirit by A.W. Tozer
  Religion/Christianity, ISBN: 9789389157215

- How to Enjoy Your Life and Your Job by Dale Carnegie
  Self Help/General, ISBN: 9789388118293

- Illust. Biography of William Shakespeare by Manju Gupta
  Biographies/Authors, ISBN: 9789387669246

- Madhubala by Manju Gupta
  Biographies/Cinems, ISBN: 9789387669253

- Mansarover 1 (Hindi) by Premchand
  Fiction/Short Stories, ISBN: 9789387669086

- Meditations by Marcus Aurelius
  Non Fiction/Philosopy, ISBN: 9789388118781

- My Inventions: The Autobio. of Nikola Tesla by Nikola Tesla
  Autobiographies/Scientists, ISBN: 9789388118187

- Selected Stories of Rabindranath Tagore by Rabindranath Tagore
  Fiction/Short Stories, ISBN: 9789387669307

- Sense and Sensibility by Jane Austen
  Fiction/Classics, ISBN: 9789387669109

- Siddhartha by Hermann Hesse
  Fiction/Classics, ISBN: 9789387669116

- Tales from India by Rudyard Kipling
  Fiction/Short Stories, ISBN: 9789387669123

OTHER HARDBACK BOOKS

- Tales from Shakespeare by Charles Lamb, Mary Lamb
  Fiction/Short Stories, ISBN: 9789387669314

- The Alchemy of Happiness by Al-Ghazzali
  Religion & Spirituality, ISBN: 9789388118309

- The Art of Public Speaking by Dale Carnegie
  Self Help/General, ISBN: 9789388118477

- The Autobiography of a Yogi by Paramahansa Yogananda
  Autobiographies/General, ISBN: 9789387669192

- The Dynamic Laws of Prosperity by Catherine Ponder
  Mind, Body & Spirit, ISBN: 9789388118194

- The Elements of Style by William Strunk
  Non Fiction/Skill, ISBN: 9789389157222

- The Game of Life and How to Play It by Florence Scovel Shinn
  Mind, Body & Spirit, ISBN: 9789388118316

- The Imitation of Christ by Thomas À Kempis
  Religion/Christianity, ISBN: 9789388118200

- The Jungle Book by Rudyard Kipling
  Children's/Classics, ISBN: 9789387669338

- The Knowledge of the Holy by A.W. Tozer
  Religion/Christianity, ISBN: 9789389157239

- The Light of Asia by Sir Edwin Arnold
  Fiction/Poetry, ISBN: 9789387669130

- The Magic of Faith by Joseph Murphy
  Mind, Body & Spirit, ISBN: 9789388118712

- The Origin of Species by Charles Darwin
  Sciences/Life Sciences, ISBN: 9789387669345

- The Path of Prosperity by James Allen
  Mind, Body & Spirit, ISBN: 9789388118323

OTHER HARDBACK BOOKS

- The Power of Awareness by Neville Goddard
  Mind, Body & Spirit, ISBN: 9789388118330

- The Power of Concentration by Theron Q. Dumont
  Self Help/General, ISBN: 9789388118224

- The Power of Positive Thinking by Norman Vincent Peale
  Mind, Body & Spirit, ISBN: 9789388118729

- The Prophet by Kahlil Gibran
  Fiction/Classics, ISBN: 9789388118453

- The Psychopathology of Everyday Life by Sigmund Freud
  Non Fiction/Psychology, ISBN: 9789388118231

- The Pursuit of God by A.W. Tozer
  Religion/Christianity, ISBN: 9789389157246

- The Quick and Easy Way to Effec. Speaking by Dale Carnegie
  Self Help/General, ISBN: 9789388118347

- The Science of Getting Rich by Wallace D. Wattles
  Self Help/Success, ISBN: 9789387669239

- The Seven Laws of Teaching by John Milton Gregory
  Self Help/General, ISBN: 9789388118460

- The Upanishads by Swami Paramananda
  Religion/Hinduism, ISBN: 9789388118774

- The World as I See It by Albert Einstein
  Non Fiction/Philosopy, ISBN: 9789388118248

- Thought Vibration by William Walker Atkinson
  Non Fiction/Philosopy, ISBN: 9789389157253

- Wake Up and Live! by Dorothea Brande
  Mind, Body & Spirit, ISBN: 9789388118255

- Your Faith is Your Fortune by Neville Goddard
  Religion & Spirituality, ISBN: 9789389157260

www.ingramcontent.com/pod-product-compliance
Lightning Source LLC
Chambersburg PA
CBHW030503100426
42813CB00002B/322